WONDERFUL WORLD OF KNOWLEDGE

Treasures of the Earth

Disney's

Wonderful
World of
Knowledge

THE DANBURY PRESS

THE DANBURY PRESS

a division of Grolier Enterprises, Inc.

ROBERT B. CLARKE   *Publisher*

THE STONEHOUSE PRESS   *Production Supervision*

ARNOLDO MONDADORI EDITORE

MARIO GENTILINI   *Editor-in-Chief*

ELISA PENNA   *Supervising Editor*

GIOVAN BATTISTA CARPI   *Illustrators*
CLAUDIO MAZZOLI

GUIDO MARTINA   *Author*

"Disney's WONDERFUL WORLD OF KNOWLEDGE"
is an updated and enlarged English version of
an encyclopedia heretofore printed in the Italian language by
ARNOLDO MONDADORI EDITORE, MILAN
and entitled (in English Translation) "Disney ENCYCLOPEDIA"

CONTENTS

THE GREAT TREASURE CHEST

Believe it or not, boys and girls, here I am. Uncle Scrooge—in flesh and feather —at your service. The very moment I heard that a book about treasure chests, jewels, and other valuables was being prepared, I immediately offered my services. There certainly can't be anyone better qualified to tell this story than your favorite Uncle Scrooge. Naturally my offer was accepted. So I'll act as your tour guide on a most unusual journey—a journey through a remarkable but rather mysterious treasure chest. The particular chest I have in mind (if you haven't already guessed) is our great planet—Earth.

Through the ages people believed many strange fables about our planet. For example, thousands of years ago, men thought that there were fearsome giants hidden deep in the center of the earth. It was rumored that these giants were held prisoner in a flaming blacksmith shop. Their job was to forge metals with great pounding mallets. This violent hammering was thought to be the cause of earthquakes and volcanic eruptions. Of course we know that giants don't cause these disastrous upheavals. But people did believe this tale for a long time.

There are, however, still many unsolved mysteries concerning our planet, boys and girls. I hope that our journey will help answer any questions you may have—and at the same time make you better acquainted with Mother Earth.

A GIGANTIC ORANGE

Grandma Duck always refers to the earth as a gigantic orange revolving around the sun. The path that our planet takes on this long journey is called the earth's orbit. And during this orbit, we're 93,000,000 miles from the sun!

I guess it would be safe to say that one orbit isn't exactly an overnight trip. In fact it takes our planet 365 days, 6 hours, 9 minutes, and 9 seconds to complete the journey around the sun. Yes, boys and girls, you guessed right. This circling, or revolution, is equal to one solar year. During this time we experience our four seasons—winter, summer, spring, and fall. Of course the earth also has another motion. Our planet rotates on its axis, an imaginary line connecting the North and South Poles. The earth spins on its axis once every 24 hours. This motion creates

9

day and night. In other words the day side of the earth faces the sun, and the night side faces away from the sun. This 24-hour period (it is actually 23 hours, 56 minutes, and 4 seconds) is called a sidereal day.

I just had a grand idea, my friends. Perhaps a bit daring, but how would you like to take a journey to the center of our earth? We can see for ourselves the elements that make up our "home." Why, we'll be the first humans—and duck—to do it. First, we'll have to dig through the rocky "rind" that surrounds our planet. This layer of "rind" is called the earth's crust. The crust is about 20–30 miles thick under the continents and about 3 miles thick under the oceans. Are you still with me? As we go deeper the temperatures will get higher and higher and the air pressure will be great. Just don't roam too far from Uncle Scrooge.

THE EARTHQUAKE FACTORY

I didn't realize we had to travel through such a thick layer of crust. I hope you're not tired, because we still have to travel about 4,000 miles to reach the earth's center. Just below the crust is a thick layer of solid rock called the mantle. It's about 1,800 miles thick, so we've got a lot of digging ahead of us. Whew! It's hot! Just let me check the thermometer—5000 degrees Fahrenheit! ! ! No wonder my feathers are drooping!

The rock in this mantle is made of magnesium, silicon, oxygen, iron, and aluminum. Scientists tell us that this mantle is the source of the molten (melted) rocks that feed volcanoes. The next time you see a volcano erupt, you'll know that the shower of gases, rocks, and lava comes from the mantle layer of the earth. Of course when a volcano does erupt, it sometimes causes the rocks in both the mantle and the outer crust for miles around to twist, buckle, expand, and crack. This action often produces earthquakes.

All of this talk about earthquakes and volcanoes makes me nervous. Let's hurry on down to the next layer of earth. Are we all together? Fine.

Boys and girls, put your shovels down and just look around. We are now standing in the outer core. If I'm not mistaken, this core is about 1,400 miles thick and is made of melted nickel and iron. Just be careful where you step. If you're still willing to go on, let's hurry, because we've almost reached the end of our journey. Just a few more steps, and—yes—I think we've reached the inner core! Over there—yes—just beyond that rock! Boys and girls, believe it or not, but we are the very first to see the magnificent ball-shaped inner core. We mustn't stay too long, however, because the temperature is about 9000 degrees Fahrenheit—and that's hot! Don't get too close, my friends. It looks awfully dangerous to me.

Bryce Canyon National Park in southern Utah. Wind, rain, and water have carved out a "city of stone." The park is noted for its interesting rock formations that have the appearance of delicately carved spires and pinnacles.

I'm not quite sure what the substance is that makes up the center of our planet. The scientists think the inner core is made of solid nickel and iron, but they are not certain.

I'm sure you'd all like a little fresh air, so let's begin our return trip to the earth's surface. Luckily I remembered to suspend a rope from our starting point down through the hole we've dug. Just leave your shovels right here and climb up the rope as quickly as you can.

While we're on our return journey, I have some interesting facts to tell you about the earth. Did you know that this large round planet of ours weighs 6.6 sextillion tons! If we write it out, it looks like this: 6,600,000,000,000,000,000,000! Of course, the weight hasn't been checked by putting the earth on a scale. That would be hard to do. Instead, scientists used very complicated mathematical procedures and certain astronomical facts to arrive at their conclusion.

MOTHER EARTH'S SECRET

I know it isn't very good manners to discuss a lady's age. But now, as we make our way back to the surface, I imagine you're wondering just how old Mother Earth is. For thousands of years men have sought the answer. Ancient Babylonian priests estimated the planet's age to be 2,000,000 years. More recent scholars suggested that the earth was not more than 50,000 years old.

Today scientists still do not agree on the earth's exact age. However, their latest research has come up with a more accurate figure. For instance, it is almost certain that some European mountain chains started rising about 100,000,000 years ago. Many geologists say that the Colorado River has taken 2,000,000

years to carve out the Grand Canyon. Other scientists declare that the most ancient rock known today is more than 3,000,000,000 (billion) years old. Putting all of their evidence together, the majority of scientists believe the age of Mother Earth to be approximately 4,500,000,000 (billion) years.

Of course, it was quite some time after the birth of our planet that the first and most primitive forms of life appeared. Fossils of tiny plants called algae and bac-

teria have been found in rocks that date about 3,000,000,000 (billion) years ago. There was a period of millions of years before fish were swimming in the earth's vast oceans. Then came those monstrous animals—the dinosaurs, great hairy mammoths (relatives of our modern elephant), and other giant mammals. Aren't you glad we didn't live back then! As it is, scientists believe man made his first appearance on this planet approximately 2,500,000 years ago.

Many legends have been told about the birth of our planet. For centuries no one knew just how long ago Mother Earth came into being. But after years and years of careful research, scientists tell us that our planet was born about 4,500,000,000, (billion) years ago. For the geologists a century is but an instant—a wink of the eye. They study the past, reaching so far back into time that it can be measured only in millions of years. What we consider the distant past, scientists think of as "yesterday's history." Therefore, they say it was "only" about 280,000,000 years ago that dinosaurs appeared on the earth.

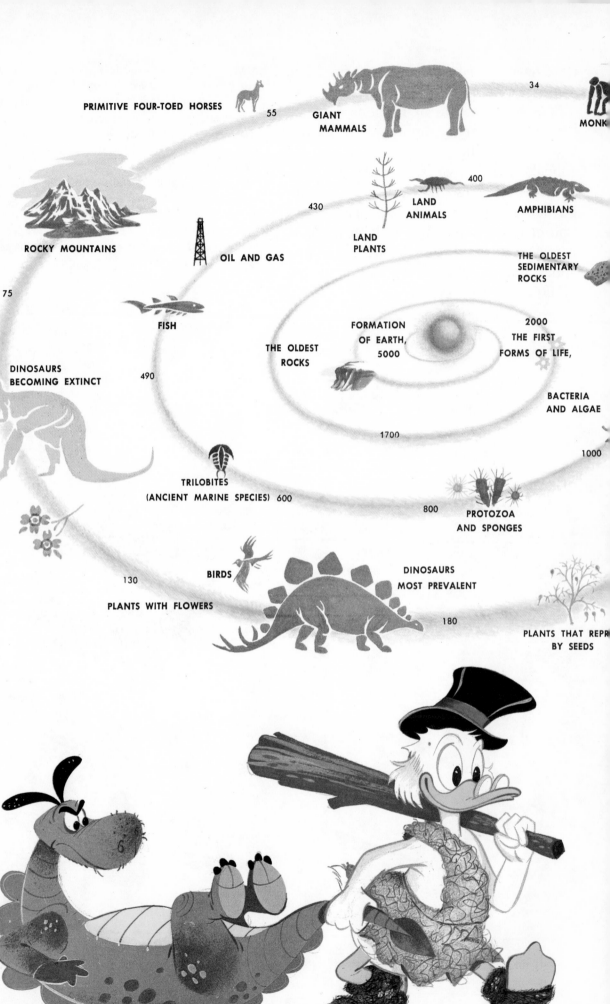

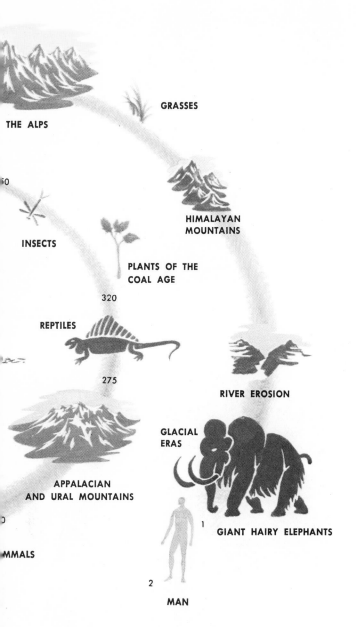

THE ALPS

GRASSES

HIMALAYAN MOUNTAINS

INSECTS

PLANTS OF THE COAL AGE

320

REPTILES

275

RIVER EROSION

GLACIAL ERAS

APPALACIAN AND URAL MOUNTAINS

GIANT HAIRY ELEPHANTS

MAMMALS

MAN

Above: Water and wind have worked long and slowly to change the surface of the earth. Over the years rocks and stones that have been exposed to strong winds and rains sometimes take on the shapes of storybook characters. Don't you think that the rocks shown above look like elves perched on top of a mountain? Perhaps they're looking for Snow White!

Opposite page: THE SPIRAL OF TIME. The history of the earth began with the birth of our solar system (in the center) and the formation of rocks— all of which took place about 4,500,000,000 (billion) years ago. 3,000,000,000 (billion) years were to pass before primitive forms of life appeared. It was at least another 1,000,000,000 (billion) years before we had bacteria, algae, protozoa, sponges, trilobites and finally fish. The various numbers along the spiral road indicate how many millions of years ago the specific events took place. For example, the first land animals, the amphibians, date back about 350,000,000 years; the reptiles, 275,000,000; giant mammals and the ancestors of the horse came along about 55,000,000 years ago.

(That was even long before Grandma Duck's time—oops, I hope she doesn't read this.) Compared with the age of the earth, man is a recent arrival. In the short time he's been here, however, man has accomplished a great deal. I'm sure you'll agree with that.

VIEWPOINTS

Well, my friends, at long last, here we are on the earth's surface. I hope you enjoyed the trip to the center of our planet as much as I did. I have another surprise for you, but before I tell you what it is, let's take a few moments to rest. I don't know about you, but I've got to clean my ruffled feathers. Perhaps you'd better take this opportunity to wash your face and hands. While you're tidying up, take a look at the beauty that surrounds you. Such scenery! Trees, mountains, rivers, lakes, grass, flowers, snow, and sand! I think it's safe to say that we've got the most beautiful planet in our solar system.

Imagine that at this moment we are thousands of miles out in space. We have the perfect opportunity to get a full view of the earth on which we live. Notice how the land areas of our planet form one large section and the vast bodies of water form another section. As you can see these two enormous bodies are not evenly distributed. You're probably thinking that there is much more water than land—and, you're right. The total earth's surface measures about 197,000,000 square miles. Of this, approximately 59,000,000 square miles is land. The water area measures about 139,356,000 square miles. And that's a lot of water!

Let's divide the two areas (land and water) into hemispheres and take a bird's-eye view of each one. On the opposite page, we find the Oceanic Hemisphere. Most of the blue water you see belongs to the great Pacific Ocean. This immense body of water covers almost half of our planet!

In the photograph below, we have an excellent view of the Continental Hemisphere. This hemisphere contains the major portions of our land surfaces. We junior scientists call these landmasses the "continents." Look closely and you can see Europe, Asia, most of Africa, and, at the very top of the globe, the upper reaches of North America. The white area near the top of the world is Greenland.

Even in our Continental Hemisphere, you can see several large bodies of water. In fact, this hemisphere includes the Arctic Ocean, the North Atlantic Ocean, the northern Indian Ocean, and a small section of the Pacific. If you study the photograph closely, I'll bet you can even spot the Mediterranean Sea.

19

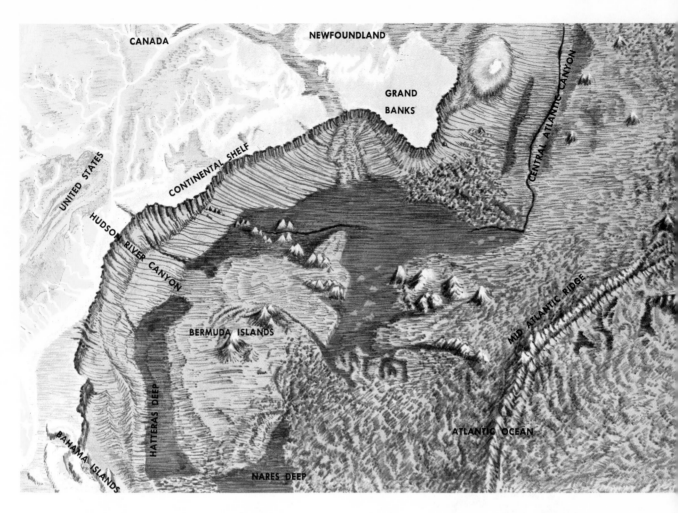

CANADA   NEWFOUNDLAND

GRAND
BANKS

CONTINENTAL SHELF

UNITED STATES

HUDSON RIVER CANYON

CENTRAL ATLANTIC CANYON

BERMUDA ISLANDS

MID ATLANTIC RIDGE

HATTERAS DEEP

ATLANTIC OCEAN

BAHAMA ISLANDS

NARES DEEP

And just to give you an idea of what the earth looks like from afar, turn back to page 8. The photograph of our planet was taken by the astronauts of Apollo 10 while they were traveling toward the moon!

But now, boys and girls, if you're ready, Uncle Scrooge has another surprise. You are all invited aboard my personal spaceship! We're going to circle the earth so you'll be able to see the entire planet with your own eyes! Are we all ready? Fasten your seat belts . . . off we go! It will just take us a few minutes to go into orbit around the planet. A turn to

the right . . . and . . . yes . . . just look at that view! Why, it seems to be nothing but blue water! Your teachers at school were right. About two thirds of the earth's surface is covered by water. Let me see . . . that leaves just about one-third left for land. That certainly isn't very much when you think of our ever-growing population.

THE CONTINENTS

While we're spinning around our planet, let me point out some of the land areas—or continents—as we pass over

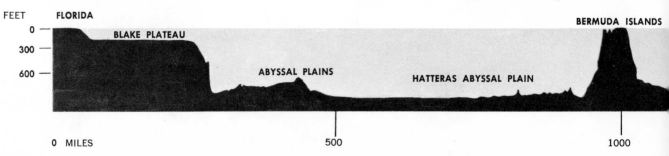

FEET   FLORIDA   BERMUDA ISLANDS
0
        BLAKE PLATEAU
300
                                    ABYSSAL PLAINS
600
                                                    HATTERAS ABYSSAL PLAIN

20

0 MILES   500   1000

them. First, if you all look out of the window on your left, you'll see the African continent. This large landmass is the home of one of the world's oldest countries—Egypt—as well as the home for more than 40 of our newest independent nations. Africa was at one time called the Dark Continent, because so little was known of it and its people.

Farther to your left—if you look quickly—you'll spot Europe. Many of the well-known capitals of the world—Paris, Rome, and Vienna, just to name a few—are located on the European continent.

Although they cover more than two thirds of the earth's surface, very little is known about our seas. It was only during the 20th century that exploration of our deep waters provided details of the ocean bottom. Charting the ocean floor was not simple. In the old days sailors used a weighted rope to find the depth of the water. Now, however, a device called the echo sounder is used. Sound waves are sent from a ship, reflected from the ocean bottom, and picked up by an echo recorder on board ship.

Above, left: The floor of the Atlantic Ocean. This chart shows continental shelves, canyons, troughs, underwater mountains, and the Mid Atlantic Ridge.
Below: A profile of the floor of the Atlantic Ocean, extending from the east coast of Florida to a point midway in the ocean. This diagram was also taken from findings of the echo sounder.

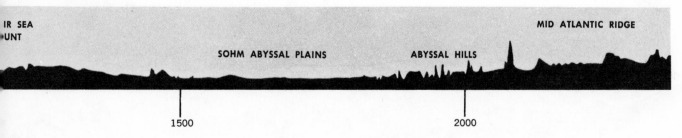

We're now passing over Asia—the largest continent. Look closely and you'll see two of the world's biggest countries: The Soviet Union and China. That was certainly a lot of territory to cover in such a short time. Rest your eyes for a moment as we pass over the Pacific Ocean. We're approaching North America and if you have very good eyesight, you might even spot your own home town. It's worth a try. If you glance to your right, you can see South America. It's just below all those rain clouds! I hope our South American friends remembered to carry their umbrellas today.

We didn't pass over Australia—but take my word for it—it's there. We also missed that enormous land area—Antarctica. This is where you'll find the South Pole—buried under mountains of snow and ice.

Of course there are also the very large islands of Greenland, Madagascar, and New Guinea. Perhaps we'll visit them another time. Right now I've got to land the spaceship because we're almost out of fuel.

RAIN, RAIN, RAIN

We landed just in time. Those thunder storms we saw over South America have found their way to Duckburg. If you'd care to take shelter in my house, I'd like to show you an experiment concerning rain. First of all, do you know where rain comes from and how it is formed? Well, pay close attention and I'll try to explain. I'll put a kettle full of water on the stove and let it come to a boil. Notice that when the water reaches the boiling point, a cloud of vapor, or steam, rises from the water and coats the lid of our kettle. When the vapor does this it turns into little droplets of water. If we lift the lid off the kettle, the droplets will fall back into the boiling water.

The same thing happens here on earth. The heat of the sun causes some of the water in our oceans, lakes, and rivers to turn into a gas that rises into the air. This process is called evaporation. Here's how it works. Water is made of tiny particles called molecules. When the water—or molecules—is heated, it forms a gas called water vapor. The water vapor mixes with the air and is carried high into the atmosphere where it comes into contact with billions of tiny dust particles. Together the water vapor and the dust particles form a water droplet. It takes millions and millions and millions of these droplets to make a cloud. And clouds, as we all know, send back to earth water in the form of rain, hail, or snow.

Let's take a look at what happens to rain and snow once it returns to earth. Some of it naturally ends up in rivers and streams where it makes its way back to the seas. Quite a bit of the rain and snow soaks deep into the earth, digging out underground tunnels and caves. Much of the water, however, is absorbed by the roots of plants and trees. And, of course, both man and animals depend on rain and snow for many of the necessities of everyday life. The three most important things that pop into Uncle Scrooge's mind are drinking water, bathing water, and—naturally—water for swimming!

Water, like other liquids, is made up of tiny particles called molecules. The heat from the sun makes these water molecules rise from our rivers, oceans, lakes, and streams. Once these molecules are high above the earth's surface, they join millions of dust particles. Together the molecules and dust particles become water droplets. It takes millions of these droplets to form dark clouds. Whenever these clouds appear nearby, we know it's time to take cover. Much of the rain or snow falls into our oceans and lakes. From there, the heat of the sun will once again attract the water molecules skyward, where the same process will be repeated.

Water also constantly changes the face of our earth. It may take thousands of years, but flowing streams eventually carve out deep, broad valleys. The seas, with their continual pounding on the rocky shores, have greatly changed the appearance of our coastlines. The bottoms of our great oceans and seas are certainly not the same as they were millions of years ago. Great valleys, plains, and mountains have been carved out of the deep ocean floor. It's really a fantastic sight. Take Uncle Scrooge's word for it. But then, I'm sure you've discovered from our travels and discussions today that Mother Earth is a fascinating and exciting planet.

THE ROCKS

At this point I have the feeling that some of you would like to ask me a question. Such as, "Uncle Scrooge, we see rocks all about us, wherever we go. But what are these rocks? Could you explain?"

Why, my good friends, that's why I'm here. To begin with, the study of rocks is an important part of the science of geology. Geology deals with the physical history of the earth and the changes that the earth has undergone and is undergoing. The geologist is the man who studies the land surface of the earth, with particular attention to the rocks.

Rocks are made up of minerals. There are many different kinds of rocks. The kind of rock is determined by the kinds of minerals in it, how the minerals are arranged, and the amount of each mineral. We'll talk more about minerals as we come across them in our explorations.

Geologists group rocks under three main headings. There are igneous, sedimentary, and metamorphic rocks. All the rocks that you can ever find belong to one of the three main groups. Be sure to remember that.

Igneous rock was formed from rock material so hot that it was liquid. Most of the liquid rock material cooled and hardened below the surface of the earth. Some of the liquid rock broke through the surface, flowed out, and then hardened.

Sedimentary rock was usually formed from sand, mud, or clay that was deposited in the ocean. These deposits are called sediments. "Sedimentary rock" means "rock made from sediment." Some kinds of sedimentary rock were made from the shells of tiny sea animals. Some were made from dissolved minerals that settled out when bodies of water receded or dried up. One of the most famous of all the sedimentary rocks is coal. Coal originates from the change in vegetable matter that has been buried for centuries in the depths of the earth.

Coal is one of the most valuable minerals stored in the earth. It has been used as fuel for hundreds of years. Coal is used to heat buildings, to run electric power plants, and to make steel. From coal come many chemicals used in making such things as drugs, plastics, nylon, and fertilizer. Research workers keep seeking new uses for coal. There are billions and billions of tons of coal still in the earth. And your old Uncle Scrooge owns quite a lot of that treasure. And hopes to get more of it!

Above: The most common form of igneous rocks. Igneous rocks are those rocks that are formed by volcanic lava hardening on the earth's surface. Sedimentary rocks are formed, for the most part, from the sediment of other rocks. Some sedimentary rocks are formed from the remains of plants and animals. Metamorphic rocks are rocks that have undergone change.
Below: This illustration shows the relationships between sedimentary rocks, igneous rocks, and metamorphic rocks.

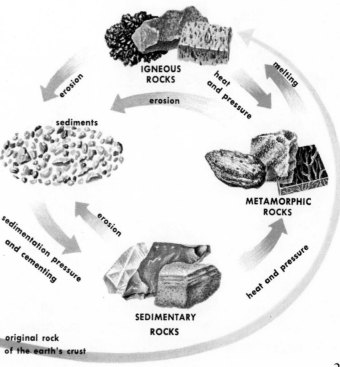

Many caves in the Italian Alps contain huge deposits of marble. Marble is metamorphosed limestone and is mostly calcite. It can be broken into big solid blocks. Marble can be worked with a chisel. When polished it gleams and flashes in the light. For this reason it has been used to make statues since the time of the early Greeks. Many of the world's most beautiful statues are made of white marble. Polished, streaked marble is used in many big buildings.

Now to the third grouping of rocks. "Metamorphic rock" means "rock that has been changed." Let's see how metamorphic rock is formed. Some rocks are exposed to great pressures and temperatures. Because of these pressures and temperatures, masses of rock are lifted up, folded, and wrinkled. This wrinkling and folding brings about important changes in the rocks. For example, in some rocks the minerals are crushed and broken into smaller ones. In other rocks the minerals

26

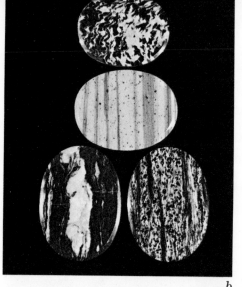

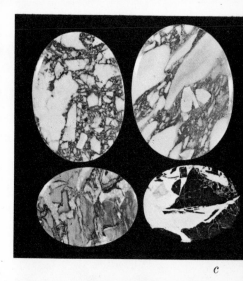

a

b

c

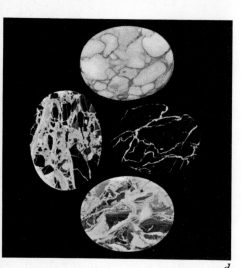

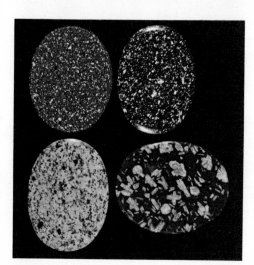

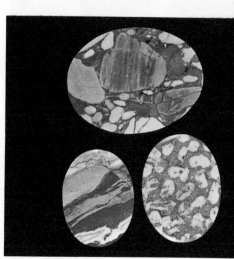

d

e

f

are stretched into long, thin, flat grains. Underground heat coming near the surface also brings about changes in rocks. Rocks changed by heat and pressure, or both, are called metamorphic rocks.

AN ENDLESS SUPPLY?

Well, we've talked quite a bit about our rocks and a little about our minerals. But we may be in trouble. Why? Because man is using up these important minerals too fast. Some day there may not be enough to go around. Poor me. I don't dare think about the day when my beloved oil wells will be dried up and my precious gold mines will be a memory. Enough gloomy talk. Let's turn the page and learn about the igneous rocks.

Rocks are grouped under three main headings: Igneous, sedimentary, and metamorphic. Here are some examples of the three main groups. Typical metamorphic rocks are:
(a) Marble and gneiss from Moravia.
(b) Schist and granulite from Egypt and Moravia.
(c) Breccial marble from Italy and Spain.
(d) Breccial marble from Sicily. Typical igneous rocks are:
(e) Porphyry and granite from Italy, Egypt, and Rumania. Sedimentary rocks are:
(f) Limestone from Sicily and Austria; conglomerate from Italy.

27

THE ROCKS OF FIRE

Fiery matter, glowing white-hot, rises to the surface through volcanic cones from the interior of the earth. As this fiery matter cools, it forms igneous rocks.

Boys and girls, let's talk a bit about sports. I'm sure that you all have favorite baseball teams and special football heroes. I can just imagine the discussions you have with your friends over your choices. You claim that your baseball hero is a far better player than the one your friend picks. And sometimes you argue the matter for hours on end and never come to a real conclusion. Actually, one side is al-

most never able to convince the other. Well, this situation doesn't happen only with sports. It has happened quite often in the world of science. For example, in the beginning of the last century scientists were trying to find out about the origins and the makeup of the earth. The scientists of that time were in bitter disagreement with each other. Can you picture those serious, bearded men glaring at

Above: A huge mass of volcanic rock rises in the Sahara. Because of their great resistance to erosion, volcanic rocks are often characterized by spires or projections.
Below, left: A landscape that could almost be the moon's surface. The "Craters of the Moon" in Idaho, western United States, are the remains of volcanoes that were active in recent centuries.

each other and pounding their fists on the table; one side insisting that Neptune had won and the other that it was Pluto who deserved the victory. Well, boys and girls, Pluto of course was not a baseball hero and neither was Neptune. Both were Greek and Roman gods. Neptune was the god of the sea while Pluto ruled over the fiery underground world.

Scientists who claimed that rocks were of sea, river, or lake origins were called Neptunists. As the absolute proof of their theory, they cited the biblical flood whose waters were said to have formed the rocks of the world. They maintained also that fossils were the remains of plants and animals that had been left stuck in the mud after the waters had receded.

The Plutonists were of a quite different opinion. According to them, it was the fire of the volcanoes that produced most types of rocks. They, too, defended their position by referring to man's early history. They cited legends of primitive peoples and the theories of many ancient philosophers. These theories and legends declared that the earth had been born from fire. The argument dragged on for many years, and then it slowly died out. This began to happen when one of the most outstanding Neptunists proclaimed and then showed scientifically that the Plutonists were right. Yes, you read correctly. There's been no printing error or slipup on my part. I repeat, it was a Neptunist who did that. His name was Baron Christian Leopold von Buch and he was a German geologist.

Now I shall try to explain it to you in my own way and I shall use a kettle. The same one that I used before. And so this humble kitchen utensil will now become famous in the history of science. It will be known and greatly honored as Uncle Scrooge's Kettle.

UNCLE SCROOGE'S KETTLE

For this new experiment, I'm not going to use water but something thicker and stickier. Let's say, something like custard pudding.

Ah, what's that I see? Are you licking your lips thinking about how you are going to stuff yourselves with sweets? Sorry, my friends, there's not a goody in sight. So close your mouths and open your eyes wide. Sit back and watch what happens when I put the kettle of custard pudding on the stove. Now I'm going to light the fire.

As the heat rises, the pudding starts to swell and boil . . . plop, plop, plop . . . forming lots of bubbles that burst and let out puffs of steam. At this point a sensible person would turn off the jet in order to avoid a disaster. But I want the disaster to happen. So now the pudding, still boiling, rises bit by bit toward the rim of the kettle. Now it spills over, runs down the sides of the kettle, and spreads out over the top of the gas range. There it slowly cools and hardens. Once the fire has been turned off, the pudding in the kettle will also cool and harden. But it will take longer to do so than the pudding that has spilled over the sides of the kettle and onto the top of the range. Now we have done on a small scale what nature does on a huge scale. If you remember, I have already told you that beneath the crust of the earth there is a layer called

Cross section of a volcanic region showing the various forms of igneous activity—through volcanoes, horizontal lava streams, and hot springs. We see here the cone and the chimney through which lava material and vapors pass. They burst forth from the burning interior of the earth and often cause horrible disasters. Looking at the rising smoke one can almost hear the roar of the volcano.

CRATER

CONE

CHIMNEY

SILL

DIKE

the mantle. This layer is about 1,800 miles thick and has a temperature of about 5000 degrees Fahrenheit. I also told you that there is in this mantle a deposit of molten matter, called the magma, that feeds volcanoes. This magma is like the pudding in my pot.

For a number of reasons, some well-known and others not so well-known, it sometimes happens that magma rises up toward the surface and pours out through cracks in the earth's crust. This substance is called lava. If the upward flow of the magma continues for a long enough time, a volcano may be formed.

A VOLCANO IS BORN

Let us leave the volcanoes for a moment, and stop to consider the magma. Because it is when the magma cools off that a change takes place and rocks are born. This is exactly what Von Buch found out and it was this discovery that made him come over to the side of the Plutonists. Now follow this closely.

As I have told you, magma that comes to the surface of the earth is called lava. Compared to magma, lava cools quickly. Most lava hardens within a few weeks after coming to the surface. Lava forms into certain kinds of rocks that are quite different from the igneous rocks that cool slowly underground. When lava cools unusually fast, it forms a natural glass called obsidian. Obsidian is usually black. Because it is glass, its broken edges are very sharp. American Indians used to chip obsidian into points to make their arrowheads, spear points, and knives. Light-colored lava with many small holes and pockets in it is called pumice. It is thrown out during some volcanic eruptions. Pumice is light gray or cream-colored. It floats on water because it is full of holes and gas pockets. Pieces of

Above: The crater of the famous Mexican volcano, Paricutín, called the "Witch's Cauldron." The Paricutín volcano was formed suddenly in 1943, destroying fields, woods, villages, and the city of Paricutín. Fortunately the population was warned in time and there were no deaths. The fates of Herculaneum and Pompeii, however, were entirely different from that of Paricutín. In August of A.D. 79, Vesuvius erupted with mighty force. The cities were destroyed and thousands of people killed.

Opposite page: Old Herculaneum on first level. On upper level is modern Herculaneum. Mount Vesuvius in background.

32

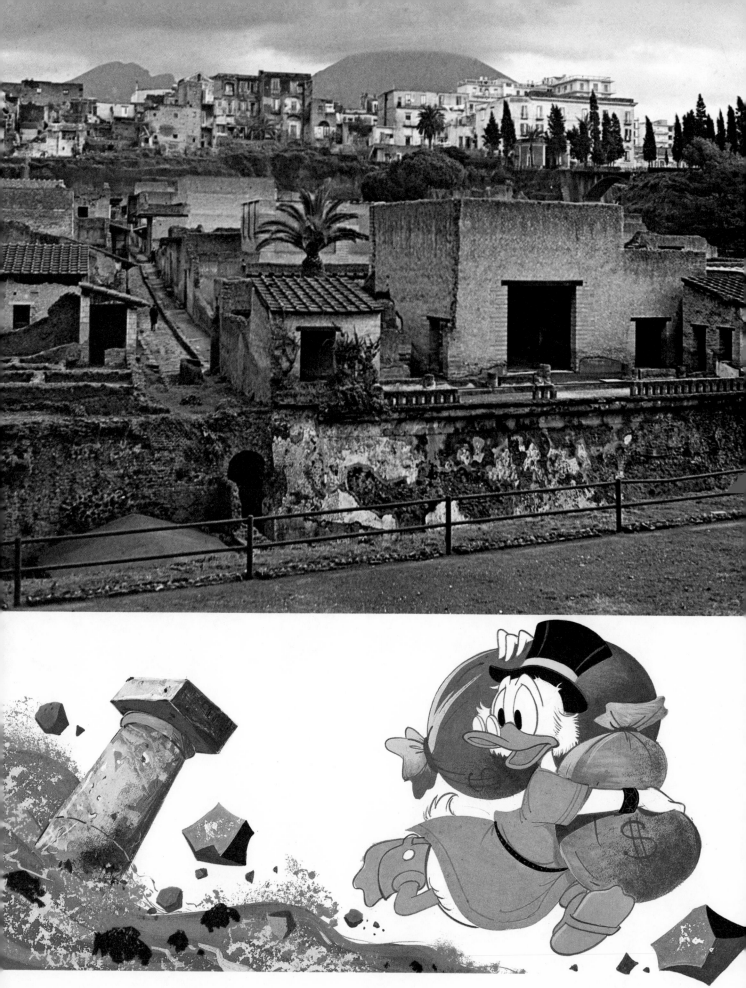

pumice have been found on shores many miles from the volcano in which the pumice was formed. And now let's get back to volcanoes and let me tell you about how one was born.

You are an intelligent group of boys and girls—that is to be expected, because you're friends of mine—and I'm sure it makes you laugh when you come upon some of the beliefs held by people in ancient times. I'm talking about beliefs in witches, impish spirits, elves, demons, and other eerie creatures born out of superstition and fear. And you're probably convinced that today, in the age

Top: The mineral syenite. Syenite is named after the ancient Egyptian city of Syene. It is a widely found mineral.
Below: Obsidian, a natural glass that is formed in volcanoes. Obsidian is an igneous rock.
Opposite page: From ancient times igneous rocks were used for ornamental, sacred, and commemorative purposes. Many artists created hundreds of marvelous figures, which are now in museum collections throughout the world. Unfortunately we do not know the names of many of these artists or anything about them. On this page we see three examples of the styles and skills of these unknown sculptors.
Above: Carved in basalt is the face of a man who lived in the pre-Columbian era in Mexico. Pre-Columbian means the time before the landing of Christopher Columbus in the New World.
Below: A carving of Pharaoh Khafre, one of the Egyptian rulers of the IV Dynasty.
Right: A detail of an Egyptian statue in granite.

of television, electronic brains, computers, and trips to the moon, there isn't anyone anymore who would believe such nonsense. All the same, there was someone who not too long ago did believe.

But let's start at the beginning. In February, 1943, a farmer was peacefully plowing his field in a mountainous region some 200 miles outside of Mexico City. All of a sudden he saw a cloud of dense smoke escape with a roaring sound from a deep crack in the earth. The day before a series of quakes had been felt in the area. Now, as he looked at the rising smoke and listened to the roar, he became terri-

fied. He ran to his neighbors and cried out that he had seen the devil leap out of the fiery earth. At first no one paid much attention to the man. But the next day some farmers went to the spot and saw a large cloud pouring out of a cone of rubble at least 100 feet high!

As the days went by, the cone grew higher and higher, and loud explosions shot a bombardment of fiery rocks and ashes up into the sky. The news brought scientists from many countries into the area. Just as they were beginning to make notes of their observations, the earth cracked open around the cone and let out

a huge stream of lava. The lava spread out over the countryside for a radius of several miles. As you have probably understood by now, a volcano was being born. At the end of the first year, the volcano at Paricutín had built a cone 1,200 feet

high. It had a diameter of about 1,000 feet at the top and a diameter of 3,000 feet at its base. By 1953, when the eruptions had stopped, the volcano had risen to about 2,000 feet above the valley floor.

The hot lava of the volcano destroyed

Columns of igneous rock. When lava cools and hardens under normal pressure it becomes igneous rock. This happens when the lava reaches the surface of the earth. Obsidian and basalt are typical examples of such rock. The field of columns shown here look as if they had been lifted up and planted into the ground by a band of giants.

fields, forests, many homes, and even the village of Paricutín. But luckily the birth of the volcano had taken place slowly, so that the population of the surrounding area could be warned in time to save themselves.

Volcanoes are actually like many other members of this planet. They are born, they live a span of time, and then they eventually die. The birth of a volcano can often be pretty accurately predicted. There are warning signals. But unfortunately men do not always become alarmed

37

by them and then tragedies take place that could probably have been avoided. Two thousand years ago, Vesuvius was a rich, fertile mountain in Italy. The area was dotted with flower gardens surrounding the country villas of rich Romans. At the foot of the mountain lay the two cities of Pompeii and Herculaneum.

In A.D. 63 the entire region was shaken by a number of earthquakes that caused a great deal of damage to Pompeii. But no one was greatly concerned. This was such a beautiful spot, the climate so mild. It was unthinkable that death could be lurking amidst so much beauty! And so, instead of becoming alerted by the warning signals, the people did nothing. One day in August of A.D. 79, the

mountain erupted. The death and destruction were enormous. Except for a few eruptions, Vesuvius was then fairly quiet for over 1,200 years. But in 1944 it erupted and partially destroyed two towns in its vicinity.

A VOLCANO DIES

So you see there are volcanoes that become active again after centuries of calm and others that are almost always active. And then there are those that die or become extinct. After a volcano dies, part or all of its cone is worn away. If the cone is completely worn away, a depression remains in its place. Little by little it

Above: When a volcano is no longer active, the magma cools in the chimney as illustrated in the three diagrams. When the cone is worn away by erosion, the plug of the solidified magma remains. This plug resists erosion even after the cone has completely disappeared.
Opposite page: Ship Rock Peak in northwestern New Mexico, the remains of an ancient volcano. Ship Rock Peak rises about 1,400 feet. Stern and majestic, this towering mass is all that is left of an enormous plug of lava that had cooled in the throat of a dying volcano.

can be covered with vegetation or become filled with water, turning into a lake. This is the origin of Lake Nemi in the Alban Hills in Italy. Lake Nemi covers an area of a little more than a square mile. But it very often happens that the cone is not completely worn away, and the remains of the cone rise to considerable heights above the ground. In ancient times castles and convents were often built upon the remains of an extinct volcano. One of the most famous of these castles is Edinburgh Castle, which stands on Castle Rock. Castle Rock is the highest point in the city of Edinburgh, Scotland.

In ancient times the shapes of the dead volcanoes, towering above the plains, filled superstitious people with great terror. They remembered stories that had been handed down through the years. Tales of rocks flying into the air, flames coming from the ground, smoke and roaring sounds. Is it surprising that everyone kept his distance? Maybe I should hide my gold in one of these fearful volcanic cones. Then no one would come near my treasure. Except me!!!

WATER AND ROCKS

Water! Water is widely known as a most powerful destroyer. But it is a most capable builder. Water helps to form sedimentary rock.

After so much talk about fire and volcanic eruptions, I'll bet you all want to cool off a little. Just as in the middle of summer, after days and days of heat, we always hope for a nice big storm to refresh us. Good. Just to make you happy, I will turn myself into a magician and then whip up a full-size hurricane for you. So let's run for cover! We can watch the show through the windowpanes.

We are watching rainfall made up of millions and millions of drops. As they violently hit the earth, these little drops dig out many small rivulets. The rivulets plow away the gravel they find in their path, or they carry away the soil from around the larger stones that they aren't able to move. Look! Don't those rivulets look like many little streams weaving their way around the stones along the

Above: All sedimentary rock is formed in horizontal layers. This sedimentary rock was then folded by great pressure into a vertical position. Left: The Lone Star geyser in Yellowstone National Park.
Opposite page: During the course of centuries, the underground waters of the Yellowstone region have deposited huge quantities of calcium carbonate. As you can see from the picture these deposits have formed large terraces. Hot and cold natural springs run along these terraces.

sloping land?

You know that it was river water that dug out a path for itself between the mountains or on the plains in order to reach a sea or a lake, carrying the soil along with it. Once arrived there, the water still doesn't calm down. It feels imprisoned between its shores and still tries to escape. It eats away at the banks, slowly but surely wearing away the earth.

So from what little I've told you, you can see how water can be a powerful force of destruction. But even though this is true, we must also look on water as a builder. Water breaks down rock into pieces of many sizes. They range from tiny grains to chunks of large size. The water then takes these many pieces and sweeps them along. It then piles them up layer upon layer. This all takes a fairly long time. In this process, new rocks are formed. These new rocks are called sedimentary rocks. Often these rocks are fossiliferous, which means that they contain fossils of animals or vegetable remains.

For example, the famous White Cliffs of Dover are nothing more than deposits of sandy limestone (chalk). The deposits are composed for the most part of the remains of animals so small that they can only be seen with the help of a microscope.

A STEP INTO THE PAST

You've often heard people say that nature changes constantly. This is certainly true of sedimentary rocks. Sedimentary rock covers most of the earth's land surface. Over millions of years, layer has covered layer until huge landmasses were formed.

Sedimentary rock often contains traces of ancient plant and animal life called fossils. Through these fossils scientists have learned a great deal about the earth's history. Now let's take a giant step backward to a time, millions of years ago, when the earth was young.

We're now in an era so distant that

Above and left: Two specimens of travertine. Travertine is the name usually used to designate uncrystallized limestone. Travertine is often found around the mouths of springs and in underground caverns. One can see the imprints of fossil leaves on both stones.

Left: Dolomite, a mineral rich in magnesium and calcium, is a common European stone.
Above: Aragonite is a crystalline form of calcium carbonate. It is usually white, gray, or cream color. Mother-of-pearl, found in mollusk shells, and coral are both aragonite.

there was no human life. Most of the earth was still swamp. Huge fernlike plants thrived, and enormous amphibians, animals able to live on land and water, crawled over the ground. Giant insects swarmed through the steamy air.

Gradually areas of dry land began to appear. For millions of years the wind carried sand and clay across the face of the earth, and deposited them on the dry patches of land. The sand piled up and the land continued to rise until massive mountains were formed.

While these changes were taking place, plant and animal remains were decaying. Thick layers of rotting vegetation were gradually built up, and the dead plants at the bottom were pressed down by the weight of the material above. Under this constant pressure, the decay turned into a substance called peat. And by the way, boys and girls, this ancient process is still going on in the earth's swampy areas.

As the centuries passed, the land sank slowly in some places. Some of the peat swamps were covered by the sea. When layers of mud and sand settled over the dead plants, new ones grew and more peat was formed.

The heavier that the layers of mud became, the harder they pressed on the decaying material underneath. This great pressure, together with the heat that came from the center of the earth, changed the peat once again, and it became a substance called coal. And I'm sure I don't have to tell you what a valuable material this is!

43

BLACK GOLD

How strange men are! So often they have fabulous riches at their fingertips (or perhaps at their feet) and they're not the least bit aware of them. Sometimes it takes many centuries for man to discover these riches and how to use them.

While we're still on the subject of how things change, I want to tell you about a product that had to wait thousands of years to be appreciated. The product is petroleum, or crude oil, and the history of its origin is very much like that of coal.

Again we have to take a giant step backward to a time at least 450,000,000 years ago. Over the centuries enormous layers of material, carried by rivers to the bottom of the oceans, began to decay. These materials were made up of mud, sand, grass, tree trunks, and the remains of dead animals. They became mixed with fish, reptiles, and billions of tiny sea creatures. Slowly, slowly this mass of decaying material was transformed into a thick, black liquid. Small drops of the liquid seeped into the layers of the rocks around it and were held there in much the same way that a sponge holds water.

Meanwhile, the earth's crust was shifting. Over billions of years, earthquakes caused the old seabeds to move. Some were forced deeper under the surface. Others, raised above ocean level, became land areas. Through all of this shifting, the heavy salt water and the lighter oily substance separated.

Today oil-bearing rock layers, originally formed on the bottom of the sea, are sometimes found deep in the earth thousands of miles from present shorelines. Some petroleum deposits lie in off-shore waters. Some lie at the bottom of lakes. In fact, one of the richest deposits

Above: A drop of petroleum shimmers with beautiful irridescent colors.
Right: More than one third of all the petroleum produced in the United States comes from Texas. Since the first strike at Spindletop field near Beaumont in 1901, oil and natural gas have been the state's most important resources. Some of these oil derricks are as high as 20-story buildings.

in the world is at the bottom of Lake Maracaibo in Venezuela, South America. Other great deposits lie at the bottom of the Gulf of Mexico and the Persian Gulf. And here's something that may surprise you. Some of the richest petroleum deposits in the world have been found under the arid deserts.

Oil is one of the earth's most valuable gifts. From it we make gasoline to run the motors of automobiles and planes, and fuel for heating our homes. Oil is used in preparing some foods and for making the plastic wrappers that protect them. And many of the clothes we wear are made of oil products.

44

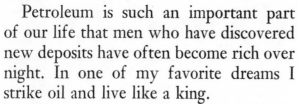

Halite gets its name from the Latin word for salt. From this mineral we get all the salt we use for commercial purposes and for our food. Halite is found in perfect cubes (above) or it may be massed with other crystals (above). Opposite page: The mineral chalk, a form of calcium carbonate. Calcium carbonate comes from the shells of millions of tiny sea animals.

Petroleum is such an important part of our life that men who have discovered new deposits have often become rich over night. In one of my favorite dreams I strike oil and live like a king.

Let me tell you a true story (really more like a fairy tale) about a country called Kuwait on the Persian Gulf. For centuries this was a country whose earth was so poor that few crops could be raised. The people of Kuwait managed to earn a living by fishing and boat building.

In the 1930's oil was discovered in Kuwait. Large-scale production was begun in 1946. Since then the tiny country has become one of the world's richest. Its reserves are about one quarter of the earth's total. Most of the population now work in the oil industry, and there are jobs for all.

UP FROM THE DEPTHS

It seems quite strange to me that the great value of petroleum went unnoticed for so many centuries. People knew of its existence, but no one really understood how useful the thick dark ore could be.

In ancient times people often noticed the sticky, evil-smelling substance seeping up through the ground. But they had very little idea of what to do with it. They did notice that oil made their hair and skin softer and more beautiful, and they used oil-soaked straw or cloth to make torches for lighting their fires. They also used it in the form of tar for waterproofing their baskets and the seams of their ships.

You can be sure that if an Uncle Scrooge had lived back in those ancient times he would have discovered many more uses for oil. And he would have guessed that its evil odor was really the perfume of a treasure the earth offers free from its secret depths!

But as you know, there is only one Uncle Scrooge—the one who has the pleasure of talking to you at this moment. So, since there wasn't an expert like me around, men neglected the precious black liquid for centuries and centuries. It was only a little over 100 years ago that they first realized that petroleum was really as valuable as gold. In fact, they began to call it black gold, a name still often used.

Until the middle of the 19th century men had very little idea of how to discover where the deep petroleum beds lay. And then, once the rich deposits were found, there was no way to extract the liquid. American pioneers had seen the Indians soaking oil up in blankets or digging deep pits to collect it. These were the methods people adopted to gather the oil they needed for manufacturing their medicines and lighting their lamps.

As the world became more industrialized, larger and larger amounts of petroleum were needed to oil the machinery, light the factories, and soon to power the automobile. The primitive methods the Americans had learned from the Indians could no longer meet the demand.

The man who usually gets the credit for making the greatest contribution to the future of the oil industry was a railroad conductor named Edwin L. Drake. Drake was placed in charge of the oil properties of two American businessmen in Pennsylvania.

In experimenting with better ways to extract petroleum from the earth, Drake hit upon a very important idea. In order to keep the soft ground of the oil pits from caving in, he lined the holes with iron pipes, or casing. In 1859, Drake used his casing successfully for the first time. This invention completely changed the oil industry. Today casing is used in every oil well.

A CHANGE OF FACE

Many of the rocks we know today are the result of changes that have been going on deep within the earth for millions of years. Underground heat and the force of enormous pressures often alter the characteristics of the minerals rocks contain.

Sometimes the minerals in rocks break down. Sometimes they stretch out into long, thin grains. Rocks that have changed gradually in this way are called metamorphic. And, as we shall soon see, ordinary rocks often become very valuable.

If you write on a slate blackboard in school or use a pencil for drawing a picture, you've already had some experience with metamorphic rocks.

The slate of a blackboard comes from shale that has been compressed with other kinds of rock and clay to give it its special quality. Besides being used for blackboards, slate is also widely used for the roofs of houses.

Now, how about the "lead" in your pencil? Well, believe it or not, this "lead"

48

is really carbon. Through certain very gradual changes the carbon becomes a soft, greasy material called graphite. Graphite is used in the manufacture of many useful products including ordinary pencil lead.

I'm quite sure marble is a material that is familiar to all of you. You've probably seen marble fireplaces, ornaments, or walls. If you have, you know what a hard rock it is. Well, it might surprise you to learn that marble is really metamorphosed, or changed, limestone.

One of the hardest rocks known is

Above: Metamorphic rock is characterized by the veins of color running through it. Marble often contains streaks of red, yellow, blue, or green. Opposite page: A marble quarry near Carrara, Italy. Some of the world's finest marble comes from this region.

quartzite. Quartzite comes from sandstone that has been gradually transformed by great pressure and intense heat.

The stone that might be given the name of Cinderella of the rock world is the diamond. Precious diamonds were born of volcanic activity deep within the earth. The heat and pressure of molten lava slowly changed the characteristics of the carbon lying in the rubble so completely that beautiful diamonds resulted. So you're quite right in saying that a priceless diamond is nothing but an ordinary piece of coal.

Above: A quartzite quarry in the Piedmont area of Italy. Quartzite, a metamorphic rock, is characterized by its flaky quality.
Left: Serpentine, marked by colored streaks, is often used for decorative carvings.
Below, left: Pyrophyllite, usually found in aluminum-rich metamorphic rocks, is made up of flaky, shiny clusters.
Below, right: Chlorite can be found in colors ranging from black to pearly white. Most chlorite has a greenish tint.

50

You might ask why men haven't tried to make diamonds artificially. The answer is, they have. For many years diamonds, one of the hardest materials known, have been produced for industrial purposes. Artificial diamonds are so expensive and small that they cannot be used as ornaments. But they are hard, smooth, and almost indestructible. These diamonds are at work all around you. They are used to make phonograph needles, lenses, and fine cutting tools.

Above: Slate was once layers of clay in a river bed. Slate is a metamorphic rock that splits quite easily. Generally gray-blue in color, it is often used for roofs or garden paths.
Below: Three minerals of metamorphic origin. Top, staurolite. Left, cyanite. Right, microcline.

51

THE EARTH'S TREASURES

I see that we have almost reached the middle of this book, and I think it's about time that we talked a bit about the treasures of the earth.

I have already mentioned how even in prehistoric times our earth provided man with the basic things he needed for life. Prehistoric, by the way, means before history—that is, before there were any written records of events.

Well, at a remote time in prehistory, early man learned to make his first tools and weapons from the stones he found scattered around him. For this reason, scientists have named this time the Stone Age.

Today we live in an age that is very different from that of our prehistoric ancestors. It is an age in which each day brings us a new discovery, a new technical or scientific advance. And yet we continue to use the same substances our early ancestors did, except that we have learned how to transform them into materials that greatly enrich our lives.

I am not exaggerating when I say that most of the things that make up our lives today come from "stones," or to be more exact, from minerals. Automobiles, airplanes, and spaceships. Home appliances, television sets, glassware, and china. All these come from the realm of minerals.

But before entering more deeply into this fabulous realm, let's stop for a moment for a definition.

What is a mineral? According to scientists, minerals are substances found in nature in the form of crystals. They are made up of certain combinations of atoms of one or more elements. This sounds a little difficult, I know. But think of elements as the basic substances of the universe, and atoms as their building blocks. Scientists have so far discovered over 100 elements, and they have identified about 1,500 different minerals.

I can imagine your next question. What is the difference between a mineral and a rock? Not a great deal, really. A rock is usually a combination of several minerals.

It took scientists centuries to arrive at these definitions. In earlier times, people had different theories. For example, the Greek philosopher and scientist Aristotle, who lived in the 4th century B.C., believed that rocks were created by the light of the sun and distant stars. In the Middle Ages it was thought that minerals grew in the earth from seeds.

53

FRANKLINITE

SMITHSONITE

SPHALERITE
(blende)

ZINCITE, WILLEMITE,
and FRANKLINITE

EARTHY HEMATITE

OOLITIC HEMATITE

HEMATITE
(iron ore)

METEORITE

MAGNETITE
(iron ore)

SMOKY QUARTZ

APATITE CRYSTALS IN CALCITE

EMERALD

ROSE QUARTZ

CASSITERITE
(tin ore)

GALENA
(lead ore)

FLUORITE
(twin crystals)

I'm not joking. Some people actually planted diamonds and other jewels in the ground in hopes of a good harvest. Of course they were disappointed.

People also thought that some stones were of animal origin. One in particular was believed to grow in the head of a toad. It was said to relieve toothaches, cure kidney ailments, and make stomach pains disappear.

But before we laugh too hard at such ideas consider this: Fifty years ago who would have believed that a mold of the kind found on stale bread would produce a wonder drug like penicillin?

54

THE STONES OF FORTUNE

The ancient superstitions about stones largely have been forgotten. People no longer believe that they possess magical properties to cure illness or to bring good fortune. Yet one custom relating to jewels has persisted over the centuries and up to the present time.

You remember that Aristotle thought precious stones fell to earth from the stars. Well, from this belief came the conviction that there was a very close

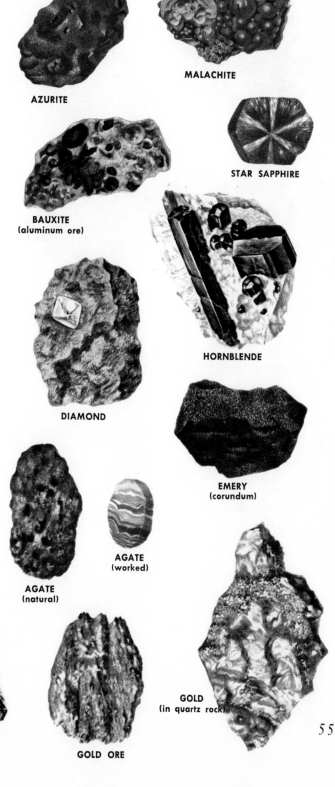

NATIVE COPPER

CHALCOPYRITE
(copper ore)

AZURITE

MALACHITE

BAUXITE
(aluminum ore)

STAR SAPPHIRE

DIAMOND

HORNBLENDE

EMERY
(corundum)

TALC
(granular)

CROCIDOLITE
(blue asbestos)

AGATE
(natural)

AGATE
(worked)

TALC
(foliated)

ARGENTITE
(silver ore)

GOLD ORE

GOLD
(in quartz rock)

MICROCLINE
(feldspar)

LABRADORITE
(feldspar)

SULFUR

SERPENTINE

ANORTHITE
(feldspar)

ANORTHITE
(feldspar)

ALBITE
(feldspar)

SKUTTERUDITE
(cobalt ore)

RUBY

ORTHOCLASE
(feldspar)

MUSCOVITE
(mica)

BIOTITE
(mica)

COBALTITE
(cobalt ore)

GRAPHITE

connection between the mineral world and the planets and stars. In fact, it was thought—and some believe it today—that the movements of these heavenly bodies can influence human events. This belief, called astrology, goes back to very ancient times.

Astrologers called the imagined path of the sun, moon, and planets the zodiac. The zodiac was divided into 12 different signs, or constellations. Whoever was born under a certain sign of the zodiac was thought to be protected by the jewel associated with that sign.

Today many people who are not at all superstitious still like to wear as an ornament—a ring or necklace—the jewel associated with the month of their birth. Such a jewel is called a birthstone. Here

is a list of birthstones for each month of the year:

January: *garnet*. February: *amethyst*. March: *aquamarine*. April: *diamond*. May: *emerald*. June: *pearl*. July: *ruby*. August: *peridot*. September: *sapphire*. October: *opal*. November: *topaz*. December: *turquoise*.

Should you want to give someone a present of a birthstone, you don't really have to spend a fortune for real diamonds, emeralds, or rubies. You can find quite nice imitations in stores at reasonable prices. I know because I gave Daisy, who was born in June, a pearl as a birthday present! It was an artificial one, but she loved it anyway.

But enough stories for a moment. It's time to take a closer look at the world

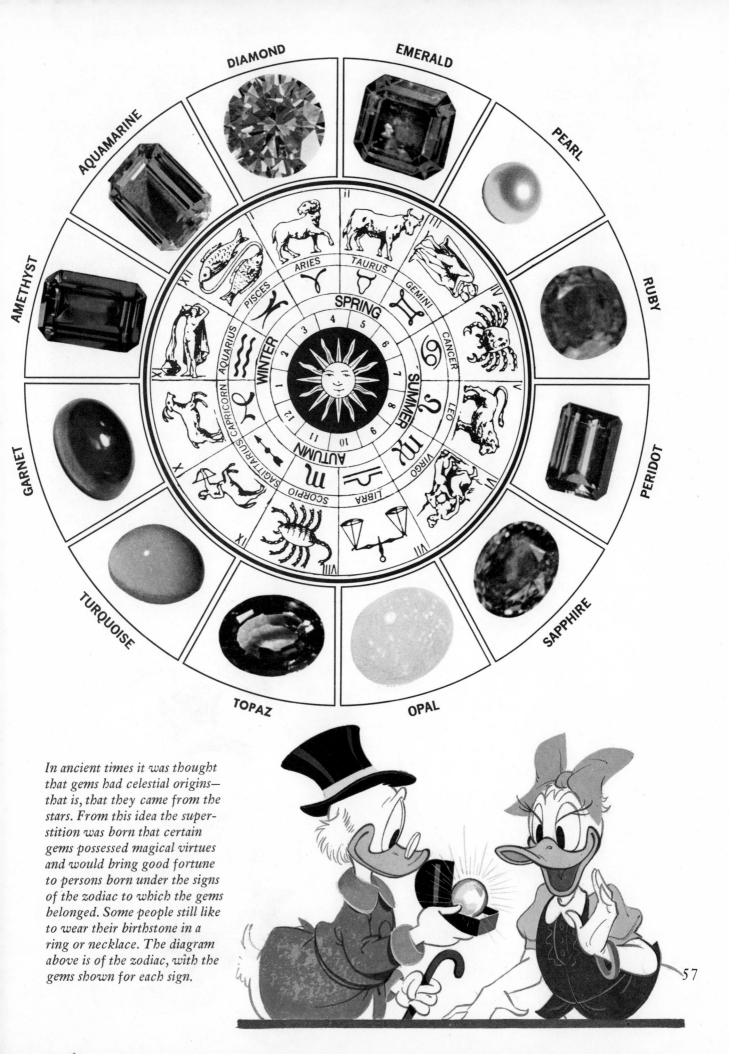

In ancient times it was thought that gems had celestial origins—that is, that they came from the stars. From this idea the superstition was born that certain gems possessed magical virtues and would bring good fortune to persons born under the signs of the zodiac to which the gems belonged. Some people still like to wear their birthstone in a ring or necklace. The diagram above is of the zodiac, with the gems shown for each sign.

57

of minerals. We will divide them into two large categories: those from which we obtain important metals and those which have no metals, or at least none in large quantities. First we will talk about the metals we get from minerals. Are you ready? Because we are going to journey back in time again. But not too far, only a few thousand years or so.

THE SHIELD OF ACHILLES

I'm sure you've heard of Homer, the famous Greek poet who lived almost 3,000 years ago. Homer is believed to have been the author of two of the earliest literary masterpieces, the *Iliad* and the *Odyssey*.

In the *Iliad*, a long poem about the war between the Greeks and Trojans, we read how the Greek hero Achilles was left

Opposite page: *A painting showing a scene from Homer's epic poem the* Iliad. *Thetis is giving her son, Achilles, the shield made for him by the god Hephaestus (Vulcan). It was forged of iron, gold, copper, and silver.*
Left: *Copper in its native state. It was known to early man who used it to make weapons and tools.*
Below: *Chalcopyrite, the chief ore from which copper is obtained.*

without weapons. Wanting to return to the battle to avenge the death of his friend Patroclus, Archilles turned to his mother, Thetis, for help.

Thetis asked the god Hephaestus (whom the Romans called Vulcan) to forge new equipment for her son. The god agreed and personally made the new weapons. Among them was a shield that was remarkable for its great beauty. To make it Hephaestus used gold, silver, iron, and copper. And here the names of these four metals appear for the first time.

But copper was known at least several thousand years before Homer. It was used by prehistoric man, who found it in its native state. Native means that it was not combined with other elements, as is the case with most metals. Thus it could be used easily to make tools and weapons that were superior to wood or stone. Later, man would learn to separate metals from their minerals by smelting or refining.

Zinc and tin also were known in ancient times. When tin was alloyed with copper (an alloy is a mixture of metals), it formed bronze, which was stronger than copper. The discovery of bronze was so important that it gave its name to an age in the history of mankind. In fact, with the Bronze Age prehistory ended and historical civilization began for the people of Mesopotamia (modern Iraq) and the eastern Mediterranean.

Bronze armor, swords, and shields were used to conquer lands as well as to defend against conquest. Bronze plows could cultivate the earth more efficiently than plows made of wood. Tools made of bronze built civilizations, and bronze objects of art beautified them.

Bronze is still used in our own day. It has a number of industrial uses, and it is also popular for decoration and art work. Most of the statues you've seen in the park are made of bronze. Polished bronze has a deep, golden brown color, but in time it acquires a greenish cast.

The Bronze Age covered a span of time from about 4000 or 3500 B.C. to approximately 1500 or 1000 B.C. Then it declined and finally died out, to be replaced by a new age.

But that is getting ahead of our story. Let's remain awhile in the ancient East, and I'll tell you about some other metallic minerals. Some you may be familiar with, and others you may never have heard of. But all have a long history.

THE EYES OF JEZEBEL

Have you ever heard of Jezebel? She was a queen, the wife of King Ahab of Israel, and she lived during the 9th century B.C. She was a Phoenician and she is said to have introduced the worship of the pagan god Baal among the Hebrews.

Jezebel has a reputation as a wicked queen, but I am not going to list her misdeeds. I have mentioned her name only for one reason, because in a version of the Bible it says that she used stibic stone to paint her eyes.

Now, stibic stone is the mineral stibnite, from which we get antimony. A form of antimony was used in biblical times as a cosmetic to darken and beautify the eyes. Egyptian and Arab women used it in the same way. The Arabs knew it as *kohl*.

Above: Sphalerite, which is also known as blende, is the chief ore of the metal zinc. Zinc is used to plate (galvanize) other metals to prevent rusting. It is also alloyed with copper to make brass. Opposite page: The biblical queen Jezebel.

61

Not only women used *kohl*, however. Arab men tinted their eyelashes with the dark powder when they went into the desert. It acted like sunglasses, protecting their eyes against the harsh rays of the sun.

Today antimony is most commonly used in alloys of tin and lead. In fact, the very words you are reading were printed by type made of lead and antimony.

SILVER, MERCURY, AND LEAD

The precious metal silver also was known to ancient peoples. It is prized for a number of reasons. Its shiny white appearance makes it attractive for jewelry. It is scarce, which makes it valuable, and it has been used as a form of money for thousands of years. Silver coins, bearing likenesses of great figures of the past, have provided a unique historical record. And silver is malleable, which means that it can be easily worked into various shapes.

Think, now. When did you last see something with silver in it? In jewelry or silverware, most likely. Probably not in coins. Dimes and quarters no longer contain any silver. Mirrors and film for your

Top, left: Stibnite is the mineral from which we get antimony. In ancient times it was used to make a cosmetic for the eyes. Today, antimony is most often used to harden lead, as in type metal used in printing.
Top, right: A striking example of combined mineral crystals.
Above: A ruby. This gem is a form of the mineral corundum. Rubies were once thought to give their wearers courage. It is the birthstone of July.

62

camera are both coated with very thin layers of silver. Do you have any dental fillings in your teeth? Open your mouth and take a look in the mirror. The fillings are probably a mixture of silver and mercury.

Mercury is the name the ancient Romans used for the messenger of the gods. (The Greeks called him Hermes). His name has been given to a rather peculiar metal. The metal mercury, sometimes called quicksilver, is the only metal that is liquid in its natural state.

You are probably familiar with mercury in thermometers. Should you accidentally break a thermometer, the mercury will spill out like blobs of silvery water. The mineral from which we get this metal is called cinnabar.

While mercury may be "quick," lead is a metal people associate with slowness, as in the expression lead-footed. The reason is that lead is a very heavy metal. It is also very soft and it melts at a low temperature. In ancient times it was made into bracelets and necklaces and the Romans used it for eating utensils. We now know that dishes made from lead would be dangerous because lead is poisonous. Today its main uses are in am-

Below, left: Native mercury. Notice the silvery drops of the metal. Mercury is unique in being the only metal that is liquid in its natural state. Below, right: Galena, the ore from which we get lead.

munition, printing type, pipes, and solder. Solder is used to weld, or join, two pieces of metal by heat. Galena is the name of the mineral from which lead is obtained.

THE AGE OF IRON

You may remember I told you that when the great Bronze Age declined it was replaced by a new age. The new age was that of iron, a metal that has probably influenced our lives more than any other.

The change from bronze to iron tools and weapons began about 1500 B.C. in the empire of the Hittites (now western Turkey). The use of iron spread rapidly throughout the eastern Mediterranean.

The popularity of iron was understandable—soldiers wearing bronze armor and using swords and shields of bronze were no match against soldiers equipped with the new, stronger iron.

Naturally a metal so valuable was much

sought after, and not only for weapons. In the *Iliad*, Homer tells how Achilles offered an iron ring as a prize to the winner of the funeral games, the athletic contests held on the occasion of the funeral of Patroclus.

Man found that iron sometimes came from unusual sources. Listen to this account from the 15th century:

"Wednesday the 7th of November, in the year of our Lord 1492, a remarkable miracle took place: between eleven and twelve there was a loud clap of thunder, with a long and continuous rumble, heard even very far away, and a stone fell from the sky in the province of Ensisheim: it weighed 286 pounds. It was a miracle of God, because before then no object of that type had ever been seen, described, or imagined. When this stone was found it was seen that it had penetrated into the earth for a depth equal to a man's height. All assert that it was the

Opposite page: A variety of siderite, a mineral that contains considerable amounts of iron. The term siderite also refers to meteorites composed of iron. Above: Meteor Crater in Arizona, the result of a giant meteor that struck earth many thousands of years ago. It is almost a mile wide and about 600 feet deep.

will of God that it should have been found."

The stone that fell from the sky was a meteorite, a piece of matter from outer space. You have probably at some time or another seen meteors in the night sky, except that you may have called them shooting stars. When meteors enter our atmosphere, the tremendous friction causes them to burn, and this is what we see as shooting "stars." When a meteor lands on earth it is called a meteorite.

The people of Ensisheim thought that such objects had never been seen before. Actually meteors have been striking earth as long as it has existed. But they present no danger to us. Most meteors burn up completely before they land. Those that reach earth are usually tiny. The chances of a large meteorite hitting a populated area are slight since so much of the earth is sea or land where few people live. In

native state, but is mixed with other chemical compounds.

In fact, aluminum was so expensive that it was considered a precious metal, like silver. The French emperor Napoleon III even used knives, forks, and spoons made of aluminum.

It was not until 1886 that an inexpensive method was found to refine aluminum from its chief mineral ore, bauxite. This discovery was due to the work of two men, an American, Charles Hall, and a Frenchman, Paul Heroúlt. Following Hall and Heroúlt's discovery, aluminum became one of the most widely used metals in industry.

Aluminum has several valuable properties. It is very light in weight, which makes it ideal for use in airplanes. It will not rust and it is an excellent conductor of electricity and heat. Take a look in your kitchen. Your mother most likely has some pots and pans made of aluminum.

the past, though, some giant meteorites have left enormous craters. Many of the meteorites have been found to be rich in—yes, iron!

Iron reigned supreme for many centuries, until it too gave way to another metal, steel. The Age of Steel began in the second half of the 19th century, when an Englishman, Henry Bessemer, devised a practical way to make steel from iron. The first steel products were the railroad tracks that spanned the American continent. Today it would take me pages to list all the uses for steel.

ALUMINUM

Aluminum is the most abundant metal found in the earth. In spite of this its existence was not known until the beginning of the 19th century. And when it was finally isolated, it was very difficult to produce and very expensive. This is because aluminum is never found in its

A USEFUL DEVIL AND GOBLIN

Great discoveries are often made by mistake and useful materials are sometimes neglected because no one recognizes their value. Such is the case with the two metals I'm going to tell you about.

Opposite page, left: Hematite, the principal ore of iron. The world's richest deposits are found in the United States, Canada, the Soviet Union, France, Venezuela, and Brazil.

Opposite page, right: Pyrite, which is used chiefly to obtain sulfur for the preparation of sulfuric acid. It has a bright yellow appearance that has fooled unwary prospectors into thinking it was gold. Hence, its nickname "fool's gold."

Top, left: Kaolinite, the mineral from which we get kaolin, a kind of clay. It is used to make china and porcelain.

Top, right: Bauxite, the chief ore of aluminum. It takes its name from the town of Les Baux in France, where it was first mined. Aluminum is one of the most important metals used today. It has several useful properties: it does not rust and it is strong and light in weight.

Below: Corundum is used as an abrasive for grinding. In hardness it is exceeded only by diamonds. An impure form of the mineral is called emery. Rubies and sapphires are a variety of corundum.

The story of the first goes back to the Middle Ages. Miners in Germany looking for deposits of copper found an ore that they thought contained a new kind of copper. (An ore, by the way, is any mineral from which metals are obtained.)

The ore was not copper. The miners found no practical value for it, and besides it made them ill. In their ignorance and superstition, they considered it the work of the devil. Since the devil was sometimes called Old Nick, the German miners gave the strange metal the name *kupfer nickel*, or "devil's copper."

In the 18th century a Swedish chemist, Axel Cronstedt, renamed the new metal nickel, and it is under this name that we know it today.

It took time before large enough deposits of nickel were found and an easy method of extracting the metal from the ore discovered. We now use nickel mainly in alloys for hardening metals and, of course, in 5-cent pieces, which are about 25 percent nickel.

Now, take a look at the photograph of the vase on this page. It is one of the almost priceless vases called Ming, after

the dynasty that ruled China from the 14th to the 17th century. The Chinese obtained that splendid blue color from a metal whose history is as "devilish" as nickel.

Miners in the Harz Mountains of Germany in the Middle Ages gave the metal its name. While heating a certain ore at very high temperature they found that poisonous gases were given off, almost as if they were rising from the depths of the earth. They called it *kobold*, which is German for "goblin," a mischievous or evil spirit. We now know the metal as cobalt. Like nickel it is used as an alloy to harden metals, particularly steel. It is also used, as the Chinese used it, to make paints and pigments.

THE HEAVENLY INFLUENCE

Your Uncle Scrooge has to confess to two great lifelong ambitions: the first is to live as long as possible and the second is to own great rivers and mountains of gold!

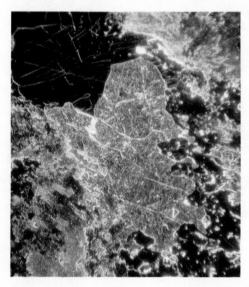

Below: Smaltite, an important mineral source of cobalt. When it is pure it contains almost 30 percent cobalt. The most important use of this metal is in steel alloys.

Left: Pentlandite, a principal ore of nickel. It is found in basic rocks.
Above: Niccolite, which is also a source of nickel.

Well, I have discovered that I am not alone. It seems that man has had these same desires for many centuries and has tried to turn them into reality.

I have already mentioned that ancient peoples believed that the stars and planets influenced human events. This belief, which began in the region we now call the Middle East, is called astrology.

The early astrologers maintained that there were, so to speak, two worlds: the larger world of the stars and planets and the smaller world of men. A very close relationship was thought to exist between the two worlds, so that the events of one would be reflected in the other.

Now let us follow the reasoning of the astrologers further. Each metal, they said, is related to a particular heavenly body. Gold, being the most nearly perfect metal, was related to the sun, the most nearly perfect of the heavenly bodies. The less perfect metals were silver, which was related to the moon, copper to Venus, lead to Saturn, iron to Mars, tin to Jupiter, and mercury (of course) to Mercury.

Now you've probably noticed two things. A lot of metals are missing, and so are a number of planets. But you must remember that ancient scholars did not know all that we have since learned. Of the nine known planets in our solar system, Uranus and Neptune were not discovered until the 18th and 19th centuries. And Pluto, the planet farthest from the sun, was not discovered until the 20th century.

THE GOLDEN SEARCH

It would be wonderful, wouldn't it, if we could make gold as easily as we do pots and pans? Gold has always been considered one of the most precious metals, for there is relatively little of it. And when something is in short supply, it is in great demand.

So it is not surprising that over the centuries men dreamed of turning the "less perfect" but more plentiful metals into gold.

This dream was one of the reasons why the study of alchemy was born. Alchemy, which comes from Greek and Arabic words, means to transform metals. Its study spread to Europe during the Middle Ages. Alchemists believed that the substance which would transform lesser metals into gold would also provide immortality—the ability to live forever.

A medieval alchemist at work. The alchemists sought a substance that would turn lesser metals into gold and prolong life. Despite false assumptions and errors, alchemists made some valuable discoveries in chemistry.

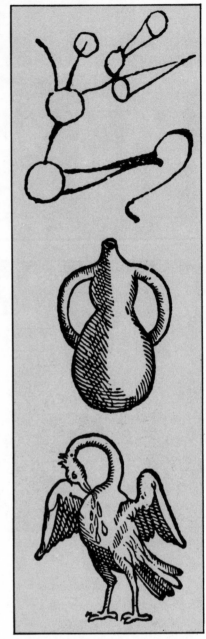

Scientists today call alchemy a pseudo-science—that is, a false science. And it is true that there were many alchemists who were frauds and swindlers. One of the most famous, or infamous, was an Italian, Giuseppe Balsamo, who called himself Count Cagliostro. He fooled many people into believing that he was over 2,000 years old, and that his long life was due to a magic substance he had invented. Balsamo ended his career in prison.

Above left, top, and bottom: Alchemist's laboratories. Note the similarity of some of their equipment to that used by chemists.
Above: The mysterious symbol of the philosopher's stone (top), which the alchemists hoped would transform certain metals into gold. The pelican laboratory apparatus (center) used by alchemists. And the bird (bottom) that gave the apparatus its name. A legend tells that the pelican tore at its breast to feed its young with its own blood.
Opposite page: A beam of light generated by the bombardment of matter by nuclear particles in an early cyclotron.

But we must remember that alongside the swindlers and dreamers, serious scholars also practiced alchemy. These men did make some truly scientific discoveries, often by accident. And to them we also owe the discovery of some of the laboratory equipment we now use in the study of chemistry.

But what of the alchemist's dream of transforming metals?

Of course they never discovered a way to turn one metal into another. Does this mean that they were completely wrong in their ideas?

No, because in laboratory experiments modern science has succeeded in transforming one substance into another by bombarding it with nuclear particles.

I wonder what the old alchemists would think of that?

GOLD! GOLD! GOLD!

California. . . . 1848. . . . Along the banks of the American River, a small pebble sparkles in the bright sunlight. The glitter strikes the eye of James Marshall. He picks up the pebble. . . . His eyes widen. . . . Is it. . . . Gold?

Let me ask you a question, boys and girls. What would you do if one day you came across a shiny yellow stone? You might think to yourself, "Why this could be gold!" And if it turned out to be true, you would probably leap for joy and shout, "Gold, gold—I've discovered gold!"

Of course you would. So would I. My goodness, the mere thought of gold makes

my hands tremble and my heart beat faster.

Well, that's just about what happened to a man named James W. Marshall on the morning of January 24, 1848. Marshall was helping to build a sawmill on California land belonging to Captain John A. Sutter. Suddenly his sharp eyes caught sight of a shiny pebble. He reached down and picked it up. It was heavy and when

Above: Picks, shovels, and a pan for washing the gold. These tools were used by 19th-century gold prospectors.
Left: A prospector panning for gold along a riverbank. In this process, sand and gravel are washed off and heavier gold remains in the pan.
Opposite page: Blow up of a gold nugget. This piece of gold was found by a lucky prospector during the Klondike gold rush in Alaska in the 1890's.

he bit into the pebble it felt soft. Marshall thought it might be gold but he wasn't sure.

Excited by his find, Marshall rushed to Sutter's fort carrying a bundle of the small peebles. Captain Sutter inspected them. "Yes, it looks like gold," he said. "Come, let us test it." The tests proved Sutter right. It was indeed gold! The two men tried to keep their discovery a secret, but it was impossible. Soon the word spread like a raging forest fire from one end of the country to another. By the beginning of 1849, the news had reached all parts of the world.

And so the greatest gold rush in history began. People seemed to go crazy. Here is how one writer described what happened: "Settlements were completely deserted; homes, farms, and stores abandoned. Ships deserted by their sailors crowded the Bay of San Francisco; soldiers deserted wholesale; churches were emptied; town councils ceased to sit; merchants, clerks, lawyers, and judges and criminals everywhere flocked to the California foothills." All of them had one goal—to reach the goldfields and strike it rich.

Floods of gold seekers poured into California. Many came overland by covered wagon, braving Indian attacks and other hardships. Others crowded on board ships, paying up to $1,000 for passage. From Boston, New York, and other ports, ships set sail on the long voyage around South America to California. There was no Panama Canal then, but a railroad was

built across Panama to provide gold seekers with a shortcut to the Pacific Ocean.

The gold hunters—or prospectors—were called the "Forty-niners" because most of them came to California in 1849. Caught up in the gold fever, they sang a song to the tune of "Oh Susanna":

"Oh California,
　That's the land for me;
I'm off for Sacramento
　With my washbowl on my knee."

The washbowl referred to the way the Forty-niners looked for gold. Most of the California gold was found in the sand and gravel of riverbeds and streams. The prospector panned or washed the gold by scooping up water, sand, and gravel with his pan (or bowl). Then he tilted the pan to drain off the sand and water. The heavier gold dust and nuggets (lumps of gold) would remain.

By 1850, California's population had soared from 20,000 to 100,000. Towns and settlements sprang up almost overnight. San Francisco, which had been a village of a few hundred people, became a city of over 25,000. Not all of the new-comers were Americans. There were Frenchmen, Germans, Australians, Canadians, South Americans, Chinese, and Malays—people of many nationalities and races.

They came to find gold, but many found disappointment instead. A lucky few became millionaires. But they were the exceptions. Most prospectors found only small amounts of gold. Others searched for months without finding a single nugget. The people who profited the most were those who opened up hotels, stores, saloons, and gambling casinos.

The prospector's life was hard—and expensive. Prices went sky high. A horse worth $20 was sold for $200. Flour cost as much as $5 a pound. The gold hunter also had to face bandits and claim jumpers —men who tried to take over a prospector's gold diggings by force or fraud. We've seen situations like that in Western movies, haven't we, boys and girls?

By the mid-1850's most of the surface gold had been panned. Without machinery, the prospectors were unable to dig

After draining off water and sand, the lucky gold prospector might find a shiny gold nugget remaining in his pan. During the Klondike gold rush, the sands were richer than at present. Nuggets, like the one in the pan above, often were found the first time a prospector sifted through the sand and gravel.

deeper into the ground. So they left the California goldfields and looked elsewhere. Gold was discovered near Pike's Peak, Colorado, and the slogan became "Pike's Peak or Bust." There were other gold strikes in Nevada, Idaho, New Mexico, and Arizona.

A gold find in the South Dakota Black Hills in the 1870's led to an Indian war. The prospectors angered the Indians by digging for gold in their sacred burial grounds. Fighting broke out and troops were called in. The main event of the war was the battle of the Little Big Horn, in which the famous Civil War General George Custer and part of his 7th Cavalry were wiped out.

The last big gold strike in North America was made along the banks of Alaska's Klondike River. That was when your Uncle Scrooge first struck it rich.

Yes, indeed, my young friends, those were the good old days!

MORE PRECIOUS THAN GOLD

Now that I have told you about gold, I want to talk to you about a rare silver-white metal that is more precious than gold. (Yes, you heard me correctly!) It is called platinum—and you can be sure that I have a few bars tucked away in my vaults.

The name platinum comes from the Spanish word *plata*, meaning "silver." You see it was the Spaniards who found the first large platinum beds, during their conquest of South America in the 1500's. Scientists later discovered that platinum was one of a family of elements (called the platinum metals), which have similar physical and chemical properties. The other platinum metals are: iridium, osmium, palladium, rhodium, and ruthenium.

Platinum is used to make electrical parts and special measuring devices. In chemical plants, certain objects, such as containers, may be made of platinum because it has a high melting point and doesn't rust. Platinum also is used to make settings for diamonds and other precious stones.

A MATTER OF LIFE OR DEATH

Uranium is a metal that can be used to benefit mankind—or to destroy it. Let me explain that statement. You see, uranium is used to make what we call nuclear or atomic energy. Nuclear energy can be used for peaceful purposes, such as the production of electricity. But it also makes possible a powerful weapon of destruction—the atomic bomb.

Uranium was discovered in 1789, and was named after the planet Uranus. Little was known about it until the 1890's, when Marie and Pierre Curie, the husband and wife team of French scientists, discovered that uranium ore contained radium. This element has important uses in science and medicine. But it wasn't until the 1930's that scientists learned how to use uranium as a source of nuclear energy.

In 1938, the German scientist Otto Hahn succeeded in splitting the uranium atom. This is called nuclear fission because it is the nucleus or central part of the atom that divides. When the fission (splitting) takes place, nuclear energy is released. In 1942, an Italian-born scientist named Enrico Fermi produced a "chain reaction." In a chain reaction, splitting

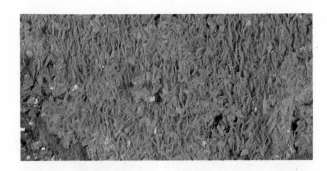

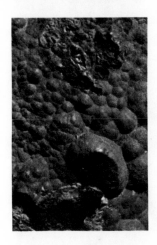

Uranium is a hard silvery or steel-gray metal. It is the heaviest of all the natural elements. Its most important use is in the production of nuclear energy. Uranium atoms send out powerful rays as they break down. This is known as radioactivity. The rays can be detected by a Geiger counter.
Top: Autunite, a mineral ore containing large quantities of uranium.
Above, left: Uraninite is the main uranium mineral. Its most common ore and the chief source of uranium is pitchblende.
Above, right: Carnotite, a secondary uranium mineral. It is found mainly in the United States.
Below: Radioactive uranium ore found in New Mexico.

Right: Chromite, from which chromium is extracted. Left: Magnesite, the main source of the element magnesium. Below: Ilmenite, found in the Ilmen Mountains of Russia. Titanium, used in jet aircraft, comes from this ore.

Below: Molybdenite, the major ore of molybdenum.
Below, right: Wolframite, the chief source of the metal tungsten.
Opposite page: Pyrolusite ore, a source of manganese.

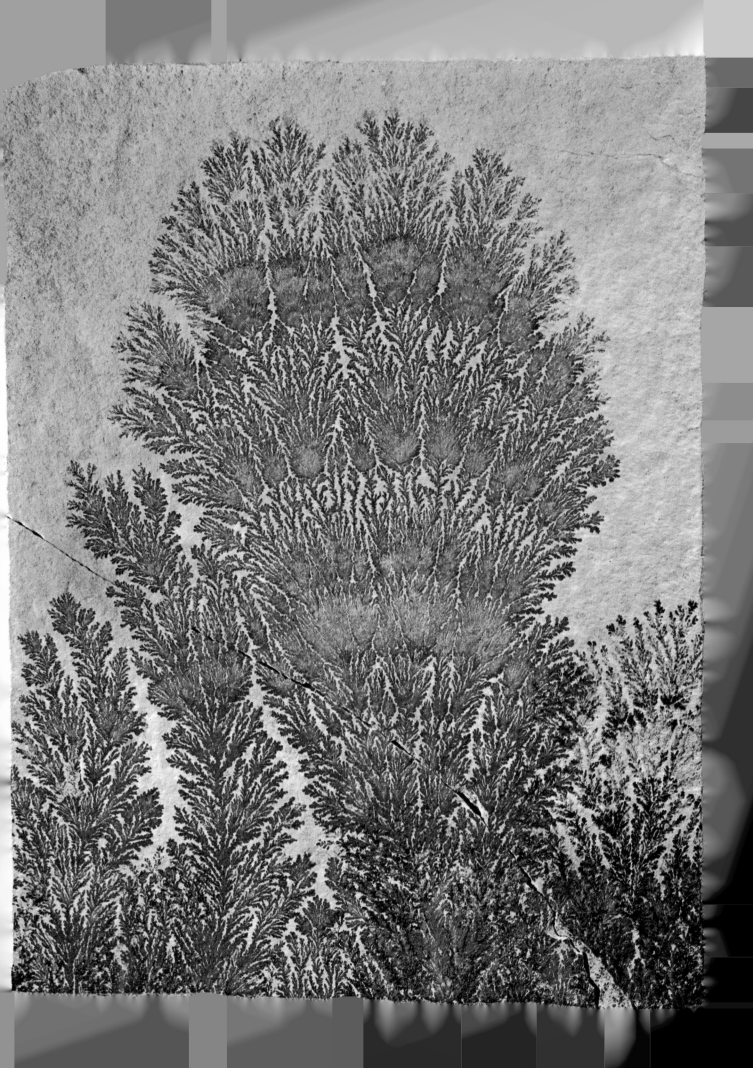

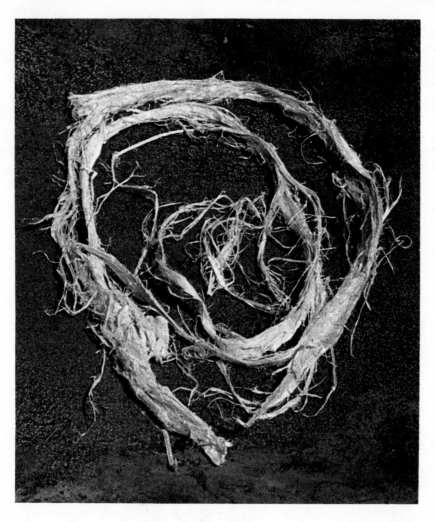

Left: Fibers from the mineral asbestos. The asbestos fibers vary in length from less than 1 inch to about 12 inches. Asbestos is widely used in industry and other areas because it is fire resistant.

Above: Asbestos is wrapped around this cement pipeline as a heat shield.

Opposite page: A fireman wears an asbestos jump suit during the famous Grand Prix sports car race held each year in Monaco. In the event of an accident, he may have to rescue a driver from a blazing car.

the nucleus of one uranium atom causes the splitting of others—so that a "chain" of splitting atoms is created. Using the energy produced by this chain reaction, American scientists developed the atomic bomb during World War II.

On August 6, 1945, the first atomic bomb used in war was dropped on the Japanese city of Hiroshima, killing thousands of people. The Japanese put up a memorial to the dead in Hiroshima, with the inscription: "We Shall Never Make That Mistake Again."

A BURNING ISSUE

Have you ever heard of someone throwing a tablecloth or a napkin into a fire in order to clean it? Sounds silly, I know. But that's what people did 1,000

years ago. The great emperor Charlemagne—who ruled most of Europe in the Middle Ages—would amaze his guests by cleaning his tablecloth that way.

Why didn't the cloth burn? Very simple. The tablecloth and napkins were made from the fibers of a group of fire-resistant minerals called asbestos. The ancient peoples knew about asbestos and used it to make lamp wicks. An asbestos wick with one end placed in oil would burn indefinitely. The historian Plutarch mentions that asbestos wicks were used by the vestal virgins who guarded the "eternal flame" in the temples of the Roman goddess Vesta.

Today asbestos fibers are woven into many different fabrics used in industry and everyday life. Fire curtains in theaters are made of asbestos. The fireman who

steps into a blazing building may be wearing a suit of asbestos cloth. Factory workers who handle very hot material, such as molten steel, will put on asbestos gloves, hats, and aprons. Brake linings in cars are made of asbestos as protection against heat caused by friction. And asbestos is also wrapped around pipes and boilers to prevent too much loss of heat. As a matter of fact, all of my money bags are made of asbestos. After all, I wouldn't want those $100 bills to go up in flames!

NONMETALLIC MINERALS

Well, boys and girls, now we have entered the area of nonmetallic minerals—those containing no metal or very little metal. These minerals are just as important as the metallic minerals. I will mention a few to give you some idea of what I mean.

Take sulfur, for example. Sulfur is found in eggs and in plant foods that are important to human beings and animals.

Sulfur is a nonmetallic element used
to make many chemical compounds.
Sulfur is found in nearly all plants
and animals and in many minerals
and rocks. Above: Melted sulfur is
pumped into a vat at a sulfur mine.

Opposite page: The Grotto of Neptune, near Cape Caccia on the Italian
island of Sardinia. Stalactites hanging
from roof are deposits of calcium
carbonate (calcite), used in cement.

87

Left: Graphite, one of the natural forms of carbon. As opposed to diamond (hard carbon), graphite is very soft. Far left: Sulfur in crystallized form. Below: A closeup of large sulfur crystals.

Opposite page: This giant machine is used to manufacture artificial (man-made) diamonds. For many years scientists tried to duplicate the natural conditions under which carbon is changed into diamonds. In 1955, the General Electric Company laboratories in Schenectady, New York, successfully produced artificial diamonds.

*Left: An example of a stalagmite.
Stalagmites and stalactites are
deposits of calcium carbonate
(calcite) that form in caves as a
result of dripping water containing calceous material. Stalactites hang from the roof and
walls of a cave while stalagmites
form on the cavern floor.*

*Above: A mass of crystallized
calcite. Calcite is a mineral noted
for the variety of its crystals.
It is present in limestone and
marble, two important building
materials.
Opposite page, left: The glassy
crystal in the top part of the
photograph is a block of
gypsum.*

Above: Barite crystals often form odd-shaped masses. The one pictured above resembles a toy horse or some other four-footed animal. Barite is the most common barium mineral. Fine barite crystals are found in Europe and various parts of the United States. Large deposits are mined in Arkansas, Missouri, and Nova Scotia in Canada. Barite is used in the paper and petroleum industries and also as a pigment in paint.

Left: Smoky quartz. This variety of quartz is usually brownish in color. Quartz is used as a gemstone, as an abrasive in sandpaper, in glassmaking, and in other industries.
Above: Halite, or rock salt.
Opposite page, left: A variety of quartz called amethyst, which can be recognized by its blue-violet color. Amethyst is a popular gemstone. It is mined in large quantities in Brazil, Siberia, Canada, India, and Ceylon.

Below: A chalcedony stalactite taken from a cave in Brazil. Chalcedony is a form of quartz that is translucent (partly transparent) and has a waxy gloss. It is generally white, gray, or a shade of brown. There are many different types of chalcedony. They include a number of decorative stones, such as onyx, bloodstone, agate, carnelian, and jasper. Each can be identified by its color or mixture of colors. Jasper, for example, is generally dark red in color, while bloodstone is green with touches of red resembling spots of blood.

Above: Two pieces of rough jasper and several stones cut out of this fine-grained quartz. Generally dark red or brown, it may also be green, dull blue, yellow, or black. It is often used in jewelry. Fine quality jasper is found in United States and Europe.
Above, left: A rock containing the mineral apatite. The apatite crystal is shown in the upper right portion of the picture. Apatite is found in many rocks. Its crystals may be colorless, green, brown, blue, or red. The better-quality crystals are sometimes used as gemstones.
Left: A specimen of quartz with arrow-shaped crystals.
Below: A beautiful, rose-colored topaz. The one shown here was originally yellow. A special heat process caused it to turn a deep rose. The most valuable topaz is yellow-gold. But there are many other varieties in shades of blue, pale green, and brown. Topaz is the birthstone for the month of November and is considered a symbol of faithfulness. Topaz is also used in industry to make insulators for spark plugs as well as other heat-resistant products. Historically the finest topaz has been found in Brazil and the Soviet Union.

In its natural state, it is often found near volcanoes. Sulfur is used in many chemical compounds. It is one of the ingredients in gunpowder and is used to make fertilizers.

Apatite is another important nonmetallic mineral. Phosphorite and other rocks containing apatite are a major source of phosphorus—an element that is essential for the growth of plants and animals. Phosphorus is used in industry and agriculture as a chemical compound. White phosphorus is used in the manu-

DIAMOND

CORUNDUM

TOPAZ

QUARTZ

FELDSPAR

APATITE

FLUORITE

CALCITE

GYPSUM

TALC

facture of steel and baking powder. Red phosphorus is used to make safety matches and pesticides (pest killers).

Then there is graphite, which is one of the softest minerals. All of you boys and girls use graphite everyday in school. The "lead" in your pencils is actually a mixture of hardened graphite and clay. Graphite conducts heat and electricity and doesn't burn. So it is used to make electrical parts and special containers for holding melted-down metals.

Scientists classify minerals according to their characteristics. One characteristic is hardness. This is especially important when dealing with those valuable minerals called gemstones. Gems, such as ru-

bies and diamonds, are extremely hard and resist scratching. About 150 years ago a German scientist named Friedrich Mohs devised a means of ranking minerals according to their hardness. The softest mineral is rated 1 and the hardest 10.

It's a bit like a flight of stairs. The bottom step would be talc, the softest mineral; and the top step would be diamond, the hardest. Naturally, I intend to skip quickly over the first nine in order to get to number 10!

Before we go on to talk about other nonmetallic minerals, I want you to peek into a splendiferously wonderful place. Come along. You might even see some familiar faces in there.

STONES IN ALL THE COLORS OF THE RAINBOW

Be happy, boys and girls! Lift up your hearts! We are about to enter the fabulous world of crystalline beauty, a world that has stolen the colors of the rainbow right out of the sky.

You must excuse me if I express myself so lyrically, but you know how it is. When it comes to riches, my old heart is flooded with music and poetry.

All around us, now, there is a fairytale brilliance of lights, a wild flash of dazzling rays, flickering colors, a swiftly-changing palette to which nature has lent her loveliest hues.

Where are we? Ah, yes, this is the cave of the Seven Dwarfs, the famous friends of Snow White. They have spent their lives digging jewels from the locked treasure chests of the rocks.

When they see us enter, these delightful little men put down their picks, and one of them steps forward saying, "We nime buries, miadonds, phassires."

Oh dear! If I didn't know it was the dwarf Dopey speaking, I'd say it was some madman. But just then Grumpy steps up, rudely pushing his brother aside with his elbow, and explains, "Grumph! As usual, this one is scrambling up his words. What he wanted to say was that

we mine rubies, diamonds, sapphires, and emeralds, because only these are precious stones. The others are semiprecious or ornamental. They aren't to be thrown away, though!"

"Thrown away?" I protest, horrified. "I would like to have them by the ton."

But Dopey shakes his head. "Let's not exaggerate. You should know there are 1,500 minerals in the earth's crust, but only 16 are important as gemstones!"

And then he gave me the complete list that I copied down in the table below:

BERYL	CHRYSOBERYL	CORUNDUM	DIAMOND
FELDSPAR	GARNET	JADE	LAZULITE
OPAL	OLIVINE	QUARTZ	SPINEL
TOPAZ	TOURMALINE	TURQUOISE	ZIRCONIUM

All these minerals were widely known and valued from the most ancient times, except for zirconium. That began to have great popularity only in this century.

In the old days, however, unlike today, people thought many gems had supernatural powers. For example, garnet was supposed to cure depression and rock crystal (quartz) to stop bleeding.

What's more, people believed that many stones came from the bodies of animals such as toads, roosters, and dragons and that these stones had the most magic.

Before leaving the ancients, I would like to remind you that they used the seeds of the carob tree as a unit of measurement to weigh gems. The word "carat" comes from the Greek word for carob seed. Nowadays a carat is the standard unit of weight for a gemstone. It equals one fifth of a gram.

And carob seeds today are just fodder for animals. But I must admit that when I see a horse crunch one of those seeds a little shiver goes up and down my spine.

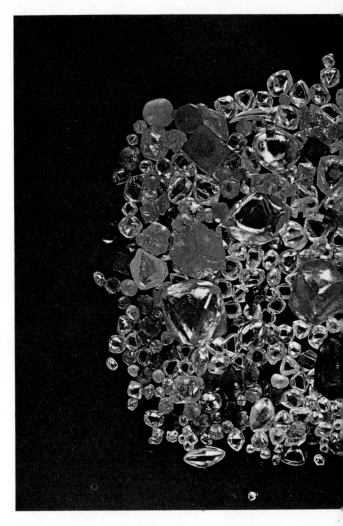

A display of rough diamonds of all kinds—colorless, pale yellow, brown, pink, blue, red, and even black. To obtain a rough diamond that can be cut into a 1-carat gem, more than 200 tons of earth and rock must be dug.

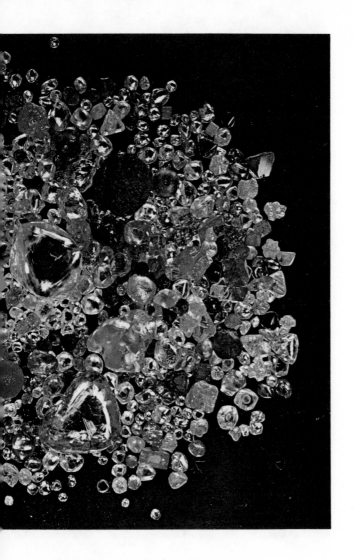

ONLY FOR KINGS

Before, when I was talking about minerals, I mentioned the oldest ones first out of respect and politeness. Remember?

Well, now let me speak first of the gem that surely holds first place in the scale of values: the diamond.

The word "diamond" comes from a Greek word meaning "the invincible one." Pliny, the 1st-century Roman historian, said it was "worthy only of kings."

Unlike other gems, diamonds are valuable even when they are completely colorless; but their value increases when they are colored. Then they can bring fantastic prices.

The most common colors of diamonds are brown and yellow. Yellow diamonds, however, must not be too pale, because in that case the value of the diamond would be reduced by one half or two thirds.

Extremely rare are olive-green, aquamarine, and pink diamonds. Rarer still are sapphire-blue ones. And finally, red diamonds are so rare it would be hard to find more than one in a century.

Since colored diamonds are so choice, dishonest people try to pass off diamonds of very little worth as precious specimens. One of the commonest tricks is to cover up the yellowish hue of a diamond with a transparent coat of indigo-blue dye.

Such things happen in life, too, when a dishonest fellow tries to hide under a coat of respectability. Unfortunately, the deception sometimes works!

101

The oldest diamonds came from Borneo and India. The district of Golconda in India was among the first and most famous producers. Even today, when someone speaks of fabulous riches, he may use the expression "the treasure of Golconda." However, I'd like to add that for some time now people have begun saying "the treasure of Uncle Scrooge."

But I do not intend to slight the merits of the most ancient diamond, said to be 3,000 or 4,000 years old. There is no official record of this stone until 1304, when it came into the possession of the Rajah of Malwa in India. In 1739 it fell into the hands of Nadir Shah, king of Persia. Upon seeing it, he admiringly exclaimed, "Kohinoor!" In Persian that means "mountain of light." And that became the name of the diamond.

Today the Kohinoor diamond is the central jewel in the Queen of England's crown. So wasn't Pliny right when he said diamonds are worthy only of kings? Well, I'll let you figure out the answer to that one.

TWO BROTHERS

In the album of precious gems I want to give a place of honor to the corundum family, to which two brothers, the ruby and the sapphire, belong. They have a common origin and that is why I call them brothers. They differ only in their color.

The name ruby comes from the Latin word *ruber*, which means "red." If a ruby weighs more than 10 carats, it is considered a more precious gem than a diamond. But large rubies of good quality and color are extremely hard to find and their number is limited. Because of their importance, each of these rare rubies has been given a name. There is the DeLong

ruby, for example, which weighs a good 100 carats.

Usually the word sapphire makes us think of the color blue. (Sapphire comes from a Sanskrit word meaning "dear to the planet Saturn.") However, all the different kinds of clear corundum, except for rubies, are called sapphires. So there are white, pink, and yellow sapphires as well as blue ones.

The most ancient mines of these treasured gems are found in Burma and Ceylon. The mines in Burma were already being worked in the Stone Age. Australian mines are more recent. These produced the Black Star of Queensland, which weighed 733 carats and was one of the world's largest star sapphires until it was cut in the 1940's.

Left: Members of the large corundum family. They include sapphires of many colors (blue, pink, yellow, green, and white) and rubies.

Above: A large rough emerald crystal surrounded by the mother rock.

Below, left: Prized from antiquity, the ruby is one of the most precious of all gems.

Below, right: The jewel known as the Talisman of Charlemagne, now kept in the Cathedral of Rheims, France. Two huge oval sapphires, mounted back to back, enclose what is said to be a fragment of the Cross. It is thought that the upper part may also have contained relics of the Virgin Mary's hair. After Charlemagne's death in 814, the Talisman passed through many hands until it became the property of the Emperor Napoleon III of France in the 19th century. In 1920 his widow donated it to the Archbishop of Rheims.

NERO'S MONOCLE

I have heard it said (and I don't know if it's true) that the Emperor Nero used a large Egyptian emerald for a monocle (an eyeglass for one eye).

Ancient Egypt produced emeralds for most of the jewelers of the known world. Emerald is the name for clear green beryl. The remains of the so-called mines of Cleopatra can still be seen. Some of the shafts go down more than 3,000 feet, and in them people have found tools at least 3,500 years old.

Today emeralds are mined in Australia, Austria, Brazil, South Africa, Rhodesia, Colombia, and the Soviet Union. A Siberian coal miner once found some emeralds stuck among the roots of a fallen tree. The Russian gems are famous for their splendid color, but the best emeralds come from the mines in Colombia.

These mines were worked long before the 16th-century Spanish conquest. Unfortunately, in the time of the conquistadores, hundreds of emeralds were destroyed through ignorance. People believed that only gems that resisted the blows of a hammer had value!

104

Above, left: An aquamarine, a clear-blue variety of the mineral beryl.

Above: The famous Crown of the Andes. In the year 1590, a terrible plague took thousands of lives in Peru. Only the little village of Popayan was spared. Everyone thought that the Virgin Mary had intervened to spare the village. The most important families of Popayan decided to offer to the Virgin a crown that "would surpass in beauty, size, and value the crowns of any terrestrial monarch." The crown took 6 years of work. The gold portion weighed more than 100 pounds and was decorated with at least 450 emeralds, totaling 1,500 carats. Such a treasure could not remain a secret. An organization, the Brotherhood of the Immaculate Conception, was formed to protect the crown. At every hint of danger, the members buried it or hid it in the jungle. Today this crown of untold value is in the United States.

105

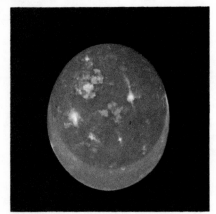

quick look showed that these were not ordinary stones. They were surface opals, sometimes called "pretty stones." Their discovery started a rush of opal hunters to the region. Or maybe I should say their discovery was the germ that brought on a real opal fever in Australia.

In 1903 a man named Charlie Nettleton, who had not had any luck at White Cliffs, left for the interior. He arrived at a place called Lightning Ridge.

There Charlie Nettleton saw a couple of opals on the ground. They were broken, ugly, pale, fit only to be thrown away! And yet, urged on by some strange inspiration, he began to dig. He dug and dug until he hit a shaft. He held his can-

FIERY RAINBOWS

Near the end of the last century, an Australian kangaroo hunter was crossing a rocky zone called White Cliffs, when his horse kicked up from the ground two

rocks with strange and shiny colors. A

Some of the many varieties of opal are shown on these two pages. Opals differ greatly in color. Some seem transparent, others shine from within, and some seem to glow in a particular light.

Opposite page, left and below: Mexican opals. The rough stone, opposite page, right, is Brazilian.
Above: Australian opals. Choicest of all opals are the black ones from Australia.

dle close to it, and in the feeble light a spectacular pinwheel of ruby-red and green-black color exploded!

Immediately he dug out about 6 pounds of the rock, but he wasn't able to sell a single pound. No one had ever seen opals like these and no one dared buy them.

Without a cent in his pocket, Charlie started out on a journey to the city, almost 200 miles away. There he offered his bundle of stones to a jeweler. This jeweler had a hunch the new stones might be a success on the market, and he agreed to sell them, although the experts all advised against it. They insisted that the black opals were just common fakes!

That shows you what good guessers the experts were! They didn't understand that the most precious opal in nature is this black one.

When the value was finally recognized, the price of black opals went sky-high. And from the Lightning Ridge mines, fabulous gems came to light—opals like the Red Admiral, the Pride of Australia, and the extraordinary Fire Queen. This was sold for a few hundred dollars and today is worth—well, who knows how much! I get the shivers!

Opposite page, left: The mineral garnet. Garnets range from a pale brownish red to a deep red.
Opposite page, right: Zircons. There are colorless and greenish-blue zircons, as well as apricot, honey, and golden-brown zircons.
Below: A crystal of tourmaline enclosed in a piece of two-colored quartz.
Right, top to bottom: Examples of agate, one of the kinds of quartz known as chalcedony. As water filters through tiny cracks in the rock, impurities in the water collect and produce the different layers of color. Many gemstones are obtained from the mineral quartz. Other kinds of chalcedony are bloodstone, onyx, and carnelian. Tiger's-eye, a deep brown stone with a cat's-eye effect; jasper, an opaque brownish stone; and purple amethyst are all forms of quartz.

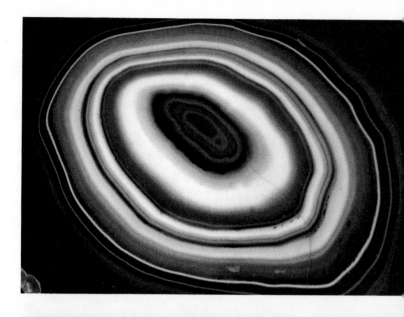

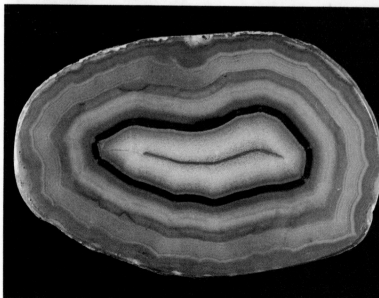

Above: Precious turquoise. The most valuable turquoise is sky blue in color and has no veins. Turquoise marked with dark streaks is also valuable if the color of the stone is good. The dark streaks are part of the mother rock, or turquoise matrix.
Below, left: Amethyst crystals from Mexico.
Below, right: Chinese jade. Jade has been used, along with coral and turquoise, as an ornamental stone ever since ancient times.

Opposite page: Four unusually fine statuettes, all of them rare collectors' items:
1. A figurine carved from a branch of coral.
2. A statuette carved from a block of turquoise.
3. A figurine of red coral.
4. A Chinese carving of imperial jade in shades ranging from green to light lilac.

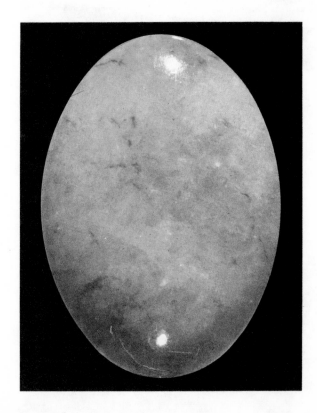

1

2

3

4

A TREASURE YOU FIND WITH YOUR FEET

No, that's not meant to be a joke, friends! Listen.

Marco Polo, the famous Venetian traveler who first introduced the mysterious Far East to us, tells of having seen a strange scene. A man, carefully watched by a guard on a river bank, advanced at a slow pace in the water, feeling the river bed with his feet. When he felt under his feet a pebble that interested him, he handed it over to the guard.

That was the system used to fish for the mineral nephrite, from which the precious stone jade was then extracted. Jade is also obtained from another mineral, jadeite. The more precious of the two jades is jadeite, which is usually emerald green or white. Nephrite is more often a dull or a dark green.

The ancient Chinese worked with jadeite more than 3,000 years ago. Around the 18th century, the classical period in China, they sculpted elegant objects from the superb imperial green jade. Today a piece a few inches high can be sold for thousands of dollars.

You must not think, however, that jadeite and nephrite are found only in China. They are found in all parts of the world. What's more, the Indians of Alaska and the Maori of New Zealand, before they even knew about metals, were using jade to make weapons, tools, and ornamental objects. The inhabitants of Mexico and Central America also used it for ornaments, charms, and badges of leadership. And they believed jade had the magic power of curing kidney diseases.

HER MAJESTY, THE QUEEN

If the diamond is king of the gems, the pearl is certainly queen.

I know some people will complain and say the pearl should not be discussed in this book because it is not a mineral like other gems. But I disagree. Pearls are composed primarily of aragonite (a form of calcium carbonate) and aragonite is a mineral.

Among the mollusks (a family of creatures that includes clams, mussels, octopuses, and oysters), only the pearl oyster produces pearls of gem quality. Two species of pearl oyster carry on most of the work of pearl making. One species lives in salt water and the other lives in freshwater rivers and lakes.

There are two ways in which man obtains pearls. He can dive for oysters and harvest the natural pearls he finds in them or he can help nature along and become involved in the oyster's work. The pearls that come from the partnership between man and oyster are called cultured pearls. When an oyster forms a natural pearl, it means that a particle of sand or a tiny living creature has been drawn into the oys-

Left: Large Japanese cultured pearls of exceptionally perfect shape and delicate luster.

Below: An intricately carved necklace and earring of ivory. Craftsmen from Africa and India have specialized in the carving of ivory from elephant tusks for generations.

Center: Polished corals that may one day be set in handsome pieces of jewelry. Coral is the hard, stony "skeleton" built by a small sea creature called the coral polyp. Coral is found in various shades of red and pink and in pure white.

Below: The two necklaces and the carved disks are made of amber. Amber, which is fossilized gum from prehistoric trees, has been used since ancient times in making ornaments and even coins. Its color varies from pale yellow to deep tones of reddish brown.

Top: Two 17th-century prints from a series illustrating how a pearl is formed in an oyster shell.
Bottom: Two very large pearls of great value, mounted with diamonds and rubies. Irregularly shaped
pearls like these are called "baroque" pearls. Baroque pearls were especially popular with the great nobles
of Europe during the Renaissance.

ter's shell while the oyster is gathering food. The oyster then secretes a substance called mother-of-pearl around the foreign object and in this way a pearl is gradually formed. Cultured pearls are formed when man takes oysters from their homes on the ocean floor (called "beds") and inserts a particle of foreign matter into their shells to insure the production of a pearl. He then places the oysters in nets and lowers them back into the water. After a period of 3 to 6 years, the oysters are pulled back up and the pearls they have "manufactured" are taken out.

The pearl's value as queen of the gems is determined by its perfection of form, its color, and its luster.

A SPARKLING ADVENTURE

There are some people who complain a lot about children. I am very sure you have heard the things they have to say. "Children make too much noise," they grumble. "Children only like to play and never want to study—and they are always daydreaming with their heads in the clouds," these same people go on to add.

Well, I do not agree with one word of that. I personally think children in their adventures and dreaming stumble on some very important things. Let me give you an example of this—the wonderful story of Erasmus Jacobs.

Erasmus Jacobs was the son of a farmer

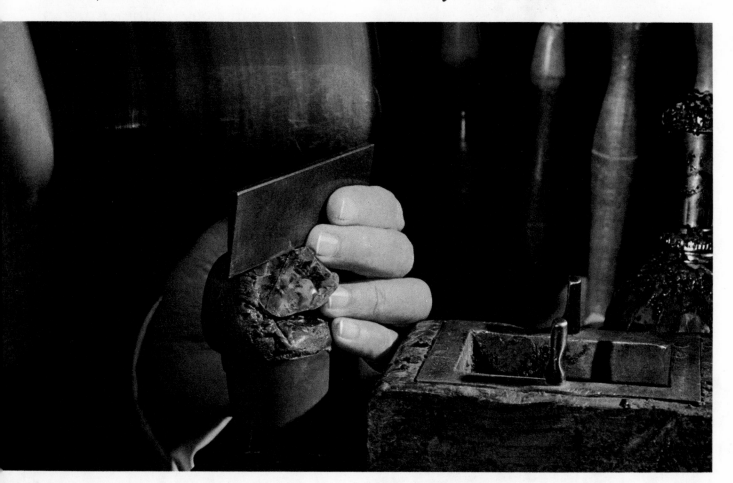

The most crucial moment in diamond cutting—the instant at which the cutter brings his mallet down to make the first cut in the preparation of a fine gemstone. The slightest error could destroy or diminish the value of the diamond. The cuts to be made in a given diamond are planned painstakingly by the cutter for days or weeks in advance. Each cut to be made is marked on the stone in India ink.

115

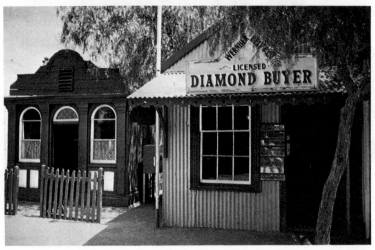

in the section of South Africa called the Transvaal. One day in 1867 when he was out walking Erasmus happened to look down and saw a shiny stone at his feet. He picked it up and found it so pretty that he thought he would give it to his little sister to play with. The pretty stone that Erasmus picked up proved to be an enormous and valuable diamond of 21.25 carats. It was named the Eureka. *Eureka* is the joyous word in ancient Greek for "I've found it!"

And Erasmus really had found something very important. For South Africans began to look for more diamonds—and they found them. Some of them were found in the area where Erasmus lived. One of these finds was the fabulous gem called the Star of South Africa. It was an 83.50 carat diamond found lying in a stream bed. A major diamond rush had started. People from all over the world headed for South Africa when they heard of the treasure to be found there.

Some of the other discoveries were almost as dramatic as the find Erasmus made. A young Englishman serving a jail term in a British military camp in the Griqualand region was put to work digging. While digging he began to turn up diamonds. He, like Erasmus, had made a major discovery. The camp was renamed Kimberley after the British foreign minister and became in later years a center of

the diamond-mining industry. In the same part of South Africa, a fortune in diamonds was mined on the farm of a family named De Beers. De Beers was to become one of the most famous names in South Africa's diamond industry. A family named Jagers found diamonds in the pond where they watered the livestock on their farm, which was called Jagersfontein. Jagersfontein also became a famous name.

One of the most spectacular of all the treasures found in South Africa was the Cullinan diamond found in the Premier mine. This gem, the largest diamond ever found, weighed 3,106 carats before cutting.

And so the quiet walk of a bright boy named Erasmus had started a great industry.

WET AND DRY

In the early stages of the South African diamond rush, the treasure hunters searched for gems in the sand taken from river bottoms and the soil deposited along

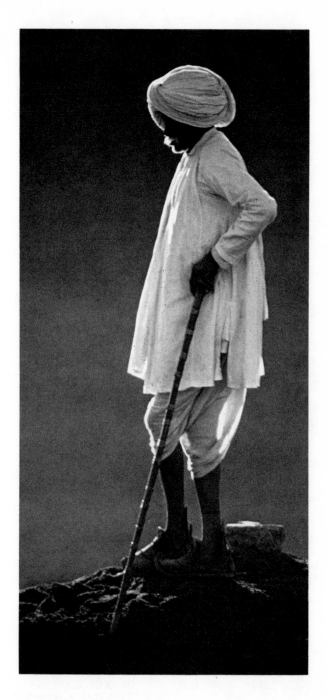

Opposite page, top: A South African boy heads home at sunset, dangling a shiny stone on a string much as young Erasmus Jacobs might have done on the fateful evening in 1867 when he found the Eureka diamond. This find started the famous South African diamond rush.
Opposite page, bottom: This diamond-buying agency was set up in Kimberley in the early days of the diamond rush.
Above: The overseer at an Indian diamond mine makes sure his workers do not run off with their finds. Diamond mining in India is no longer of the major importance it once was, but a few mines are still worked.

117

river banks. The Orange and Vaal rivers proved to be especially rich sources of diamonds. For centuries the rivers had carried topsoil to the sea and a treasure in diamonds was concealed in it. The diamond found in or near the rivers were called "wets" by the diamond prospectors.

The early treasure hunters also found diamonds on dry land. These diamonds were nicknamed "drys." The dry gems were first found embedded in igneous rocks on a plateau in the Kimberley district. The rock these diamonds were found in soon became known as "kimberlite," because of the name of the district.

THE DIAMOND CUTTERS

In my enthusiasm for the exciting story of the South African diamond rush, I may have given you the impression that the diamonds the lucky prospectors found were beautiful gems like those you see in the jeweler's window. This is not the case—although all diamonds seem beautiful to me. I do not think you would be impressed with an uncut diamond. All diamonds have to be cut in some way to be of use. They have to be cut and polished to transform them into radiant jewels. They also have to be cut to make them useful in industry as parts of precision tools and fine instruments.

The most dramatic work of all is that done by diamond cutters, who transform diamonds into beautiful objects for people to admire or wear. An expert diamond cutter must examine the rough stone carefully to see how its maximum beauty can be brought out. He then splits or saws the stone according to a careful plan. Next he grinds, or polishes, it to obtain various surfaces, or facets, which

capture all of the fire and light we think of when we think of beautiful gems.

The men who create gemstones have a long and proud tradition. Centers for diamond cutting have been developed over the centuries. The most famous are Amsterdam, in the Netherlands, and Antwerp, in Belgium. These experts may take months to plan their cutting of a great stone. The famous Cullinan diamond took 9 months to cut.

GEMS OF LEGEND

We all know how exciting it is to read about the lives of famous men and women. However, you may never have thought that it can be equally exciting to read about the "lives" of famous diamonds. Believe me, many of them have had fascinating histories. For a fellow like me who appreciates the finer things, these stories are especially pleasing. I think you will enjoy hearing a few of them too.

One of the oddest stories is the tale of the Great Table Diamond. A Frenchman named J. B. Tavernier reported having

118

Three celebrated diamonds: The first stone is the Hope diamond, a rare sapphire-blue in color. Center: The Brazilian diamond, Star of the South, discovered in 1853. It weighs 125.50 carats. Right: The Orloff diamond was given to Catherine the Great in 1773. It is now in the Imperial scepter on display in the Kremlin.

examined it when it was offered for sale in India in the 17th century. Tavernier said it was the biggest diamond he had ever seen. He made a substantial offer for it but the offer was refused by the merchant who was selling the gem. Tavernier must have been the last European to have seen the amazing stone, for it is never mentioned again in history.

Tavernier had better luck with another Indian gem, a 112.50-carat blue diamond, which he bought, took home to France, and sold to King Louis XIV in 1668. The diamond came to be known as the French Blue. It was cut into a triang-

ular gem that became one of the stones in the royal crown of France. However, it was stolen during the French Revolution (1789–99) and no one is sure what happened to it. Many people believe that the famous—and unlucky—gem, the Hope diamond, was cut from the French Blue. The Hope supposedly brought bad luck to every person who owned it. It was given to the Smithsonian Institution in Washington, D.C., in 1958. It is exhibited there now and if you visit Washington you can see it.

Brazil is a famous diamond-producing country. Many important diamonds have

120

been mined there. The huge Star of the South was found in Brazil in 1853. It weighed 261.90 carats before it was cut. An even bigger diamond, the Vargas, was found in the San Antonio River by a poor miner. It weighed 726.60 carats.

Another fascinating tale is that of the Orloff diamond. It first appeared as the eye of an idol in a temple near Trichinopoly in Madras, India. It was stolen by a French soldier. Eventually it came into the possession of Prince Orloff, a Russian nobleman, who presented it to his empress, Catherine II of Russia. The diamond was so spectacular that it was placed in the imperial scepter. The scepter—and the Orloff diamond—can still be seen in a Moscow museum.

You will remember we discussed the legendary Kohinoor earlier. Now that you know about the Orloff as well, I can tell you an interesting bit of family history. Some historians believe that the Orloff and the Kohinoor were cut from a huge diamond called the Great Mogul. Of course no one will ever know whether that is true or not. If there really was a Great Mogul, it has disappeared.

Perhaps the strangest of all diamond adventures is that of the Regent (or Pitt)

121

diamond. The Regent was found in 1701 by a slave working in a mine in India. Realizing how rare a find the large stone must be, the desperate man cut a wound in his own thigh, concealed the gem in the wound, and bandaged it. He planned to buy his freedom with the stone. He made a deal with a sailor who agreed to smuggle him out on his ship in return for the stone. However, once the ship was at sea, the treacherous sailor killed the poor slave, took the gem, and threw his body overboard. The ill-fated diamond was then bought by a British colonial official who in turn sold it to Thomas Pitt. Pitt was then governor of the Indian state of Madras. He was nicknamed Diamond Pitt as a result of his notable purchase. The diamond was sold again in 1717. This time it went to the Duke of Orleans, Regent of France, and thereby gained its most famous name, Regent. Like many of the other French crown jewels, the Regent was stolen during the French Revolution but turned up again—hidden in an attic—during the Napoleonic era. Napoleon actually used the diamond as collateral, or backing, for a government loan when he came to power in 1799. The Regent can now be seen in the Louvre, in Paris.

There is enough adventure in the story of diamonds to fill many books. I have barely scratched the surface in the few tales I have told you. The stories woven about the great diamonds of the world truly prove the old saying that truth is stranger than fiction—and often more exciting.

BOUNTIFUL NATURE

You know what fine things I consider the sparkling riches of the world to be. I love diamonds, emeralds, rubies, pearls—and gold. But let a wise old fellow remind you that our world also possesses other riches. The flowers, trees, and sky of our world may not fill your pockets with money but they can make you feel rich and happy. I become quite emotional when I look at the Kohinoor diamond, but I also love to watch flowers grow. Let me assure you that a daisy is just as fine as the Kohinoor and even more of a miracle.

Our planet, earth, is indeed a treasure chest. However, all treasure chests have bottoms. So remember the words of your always devoted Uncle Scrooge and learn to take care of all the riches we have on our lovely planet. And in the long run it is far more important that we have clean air and rivers, fresh flowers, and tall trees than all the diamonds and rubies and gold of our wildest dreams.

INDEX